EMMET'S

NOTES ON

PERUSING TITLES

AND ON

PRACTICAL CONVEYANCING

FIRST SUPPLEMENT

TO THE

SIXTEENTH EDITION

By

J. T. FARRAND, LL.D.

Solicitor, Professor of Law in the
University of Manchester

LONDON

Oyez Publishing

1976

©

OYEZ PUBLISHING LIMITED
OYEZ HOUSE, 237 LONG LANE
LONDON SE1 4PU
1976

ISBN 85120 276 4

First Published . . . . . *March*, 1976

MADE AND PRINTED IN GREAT BRITAIN BY
OYEZ PRESS LIMITED, 27 CRIMSCOTT STREET
LONDON SE1 5TT

INTRODUCTION

THE function of such a supplement as this should surely be self-explanatory. The 16th Edition of Emmet on Title essentially dealt with the relevant and available law as at the beginning of November, 1973. This First Supplement primarily contains all appropriate references to and accounts of cases reported and statutes enacted as at 1st October, 1975.

As users of the book ought no doubt to appreciate, the two-year period now covered has seen a really exceptional number of judicial decisions directly affecting many aspects of ordinary conveyancing practice. The Noter-Up format adopted is designed by way of cross-references to enable the text of the main volume to be comprehended throughout in the light of these recent developments. Also, of course, much legislative activity has had to be catered for and, although often this has only related to detail, substantial outlines have been called for in some areas—for especial example, as to development gains tax and capital transfer tax from the point of view of the conveyancer (noted respectively against p. 1091 *et seq.* and pp. 1171–1180), and also as to the effect on mortgages of the Consumer Credit Act, 1974 (noted against p. 970 *et seq.*).

In addition, the Ad Valorem Stamp Duty Tables set out in the Appendix to the main volume are here reprinted in full, as amended, to reflect the various changes in rates.

J. T. FARRAND,
Manchester.

February, 1976.

CONTENTS

TABLE OF CASES

REFERRED TO IN THIS SUPPLEMENT

PAGE

TABLE OF STATUTES

[Statutes are those referred to in this Supplement. Page entries in bold type indicate where the text of an enactment is printed.]

TABLE OF RULES

NOTER-UP

2–3 **Obligations of solicitor.**—As to the application of the Solicitors' Remuneration Order, 1972, and the lack of obligations before contract where there is a compulsory purchase, see *Property and Reversionary Investment Corporation, Ltd.* v. *Secretary of State for the Environment* [1975] 2 All E.R. 436.

There is no principle of law prohibiting a solicitor from corresponding only with a party to a transaction with land and ignoring any agent appointed by that party : (*Homes*) *Parkling Court* v. *London Borough of Lewisham* [1974] C.L.Y. 448. In that case the agent was an unqualified conveyancer and it was held that the council's act as mortgagee in replying direct to the client did not constitute the actionable tort of breach of contract. The principle of the decision must be equally applicable to solicitors, both as to ignoring and being ignored, except that professional etiquette at least should mean that they would not ignore each other.

3–4 **Solicitor acting for both parties.**—The undesirability of a solicitor acting for a plurality of clients was demonstrated, independently of the Practice Rule, in *Nash* v. *Phillips* (1974), 232 E.G. 1219 (where damages for breach of duty were awarded against a solicitor who had acted not only for the vendor but also for two competing potential purchasers in a contract race) ; see also *Earl* v. *Mawson* (1974), 232 E.G. 1315 (C.A.), and *Stock & Trade Facilities, Ltd.* v. *Foley Plastics Manufacturing Co., Ltd.* (1975), 119 Sol. J. 440.

6 **Additional inquiries of local authorities.**—A new agreed form of inquiry (Con. 29A, April 1974 edition) must now be used for all areas outside London instead of the old forms (Con. 29A, 29B and 29C) of which the new form is essentially a combination. The existing form (Con. 29D) submitted to the Corporation of London or the London borough councils remains appropriate. See further notes in the *Law Society's Gazette* (1974), vol. 71, No. 10, p. 209, and in the *Solicitors' Journal* (1974), vol. 118, p. 191.

32 ## PART 1. FORMATION OF CONTRACT

Practitioners have received a recent reminder that the capacity of parties may be an essential element in the formation of an enforceable contract. In *Fountain Forestry, Ltd.* v. *Edwards* [1974] 2 W.L.R. 767, a widow and son had been granted letters of administration ; the son alone signed a contract for the sale of certain land comprised in the estate, expressly doing so " for self and Mary Jones Edwards " (i.e., the widow) as parties to the contract ; the widow, however, had not been consulted and declined to execute the conveyance. Brightman, J., (1) found it established that one of two executors could without the concurrence of the other enter into a contract binding the deceased's estate to sell land, freehold or leasehold, although completion would require a court order ; (2) assumed without deciding that the same applied to one of two

PAGE
**32
contd.** administrators ; (3) held that the son had not purported to bind the estate without the widow's concurrence but warranted to contract with her authority and that since this was false there was no contract to be specifically enforced. Although the disappointed purchaser might sue the son for breach of warranty of authority, clearly its position would have been stronger had the son simply signed the contract on his own account, for then the contract would have bound the estate and any co-personal representatives whether they liked it or not. As to signature by all named parties, see also *Beck* v. *Box* (1973), 231 E.G. 1295, noted against p. 38. And compare *Watts* v. *Spence* [1975] 2 W.L.R. 1039, noted against p. 91, and see *Spiro* v. *Lintern* [1973] 1 W.L.R. 1002, noted against p. 376.

33   **Certainty of terms.**—In *Courtney, Ltd.* v. *Tolaini Bros., Ltd.* [1975] 1 W.L.R. 297 the Court of Appeal considered an agreement to " negotiate fair and reasonable contract sums " in respect of certain development projects and decided that no contract had been concluded since there was no agreement on the price or on any method by which the price was to be calculated. The court also rejected the proposition that there might be any enforceable contract to negotiate. The primary decision seems inconsistent with the approach adopted in *Brown* v. *Gould* [1972] Ch. 53 (referred to in the main text), which case was cited in argument but not dealt with in the judgments. However, that approach was quoted and followed by Oliver, J., in *Bushwall Properties, Ltd.* v. *Vortex Properties, Ltd.* [1975] 2 All E.R. 214, where the agreement was for the sale of $51\frac{1}{2}$ acres of land for £500,000 payable in three unequal instalments over two years and it was provided that on each payment " a proportionate part of the land shall be released " ; in the result, the submission was rejected that the contract failed because of the uncertainty of meaning of the word " proportionate." The learned judge said (at p. 222 b/c) " I should be sorry to think that I am compelled to treat what appears to me to be a sensible agreement, clearly intended to have contractual force, as incapable of enforcement on the ground of uncertainty." He held that the part released ought to be proportionate to the sum paid and that the purchaser should be entitled to select the particular area. Interestingly enough, it was indicated *obiter* that a contractual formula such as " a reasonable price " or " a fair market price " would provide the requisite certainty of terms (see at pp. 219 e/f and 221 f/g ; *Courtney, Ltd.* v. *Tolaini Bros., Ltd., ante*, was decided contemporaneously and so neither reported nor cited).

34–35   *Conditional.*—The position where there has been a binding contract subject to an agreed condition has been examined in a number of recent cases. In *Heron Garage Properties, Ltd.* v. *Moss* [1974] 1 W.L.R. 148 there was a contract for the sale for £90,000 of property for development made conditional upon the purchaser obtaining planning permission for an agreed lay-out within a specified time ; planning permission was not so obtained and the purchaser wrote purporting to waive the condition and calling for completion ; the vendor replied terminating the contract and returning the deposit ; the purchaser sought specific performance.

On the important question of waiver, Brightman, J., made the following restrictive statement (at p. 153 F/G) :—

> " Without seeking to define the precise limits within which a contracting party seeking specific performance may waive a stipulation on the ground that it is intended only for his benefit, it seems to me that in general the proposition only applies where the stipulation is in terms for the exclusive benefit of the plaintiff because it is a power or right vested by the contract in him alone . . . or where the stipulation is by inevitable implication for the benefit of him alone . . . If it is not obvious on the face of the contract that the stipulation is for the exclusive benefit of the party seeking to eliminate it then in my opinion it cannot be struck out unilaterally. I do not think that the court should conduct an inquiry outside the terms of the contract to ascertain where in all the circumstances the benefit lies if the parties have not concluded the matter on the face of the agreement they have signed."

He also added the suggestion that a condition could not be waived if it was inextricably mixed up with other parts of the transaction from which it could not be severed. Accordingly, since on the contract and the facts the condition in the case was not exclusively for the benefit of the purchaser (the development would have benefited the vendor's adjoining land), no unilateral waiver was possible. This decision was followed by Whitford, J., in *Federated Homes, Ltd.* v. *Turner* (1974), 233 E.G. 845 (also concerning a condition as to planning permission). Compare, however, *Usanga* v. *Bishop* (1974), 232 E.G. 835, where there was found to be a binding contract subject to two conditions: first, that some ground floor tenants should leave, and second, that a mortgage for £4,500 should be obtained. Templeman, J., ordered specific performance on the basis that the second condition had been fulfilled and that the first had been waived. The other decisions were not considered but presumably the condition could be regarded as patently for the purchaser's benefit within the quoted principles. Also reference should be made to *Aquis Estates, Ltd.* v. *Minton* (1974), 119 Sol. J. 99, and *Cutts* v. *Heron Garage Properties, Ltd.* (1974), 232 E.G. 459, each of which primarily concerned the precise construction of individually worded conditions in effect for satisfactory replies to local searches and inquiries. Note that in the former case, Walton, J., is reported as observing : " The plaintiffs might lose their rights by waiver, but there was nothing here to bring about such waiver ", and that in neither case was any consideration given to the point that the contracts themselves might fail for uncertainty (cp. *Smith and Olley* v. *Townsend* (1949), 1 P. & C.R. 28, cited in main text, p. 33). See also an article " Sale of Land ' Subject to Planning Permission ' " by H. W. Wilkinson in *Conveyancer N.S.* (1974), vol. 38, p. 77 *et seq.*, and a case note by R. J. Smith at [1974] *Cambridge Law Journal*, pp. 211–214 which incidentally questions whether a conditional contract may be protected by registration of a caution under the L.R.A. 1925 or as an estate contract under the L.C.A. 1972 before fulfilment of the condition.

PAGE
35–38   **Subject to contract.**—The important cases of *Law* v. *Jones* and
Tiverton Estates, Ltd. v. *Wearwell, Ltd.* (considered in the main text
at p. 36) have now been more fully reported at [1974] Ch. 112 and
[1975] Ch. 146 respectively.   It should be observed that the latter,
practically convenient decision has since been followed at first instance
in *Jones* v. *Morgan* (1973), *The Times*, 11th December, which
also illustrated a reviving readiness in the courts to find that *oral*
agreements for the sale of land are *by implication* made " subject to
contract ".   Further clear authority for this approach, whereby the
parties/clients, having orally agreed on the price and the property,
will nonetheless be held not to have intended to enter into a binding
contract, may be found even more recently in *Pateman* v. *Pay* (1974),
232 E.G. 457, and *Damm* v. *Herrtage* (1974), 234 E.G. 365 (each
involving consequently unsuccessful anti-gazumping devices ; but
cp. *Farrell* v. *Green* (1974), 232 E.G. 587, noted against pp. 45–46).
Reference may be made to full notes in *Conveyancer N.S.* (1975),
vol. 39, at p. 229.   See also *Glessing* v. *Green* [1975] 1 W.L.R. 863
(C.A.) at p. 865B to the same effect.   It will be appreciated that
in these circumstances there should be no question of inadvertently
constituting a memorandum of any prior oral contract within *Law* v.
Jones, ante, even if the case has survived the *Tiverton* (*ante*) decision.

However, most recently in *Tweddell* v. *Henderson* [1975]
2 All E.R. 1096 Plowman, V.-C., was not apparently aware of these
authorities and took a different view of a crucial meeting at which it
was alleged by the plaintiff an oral contract was made.   He said
(at pp. 1099–1100) :

" The defendant, although he admitted in cross-examination that
he agreed to sell the bungalow to the plaintiff for £8,700, did not
think that in doing so he was committing himself irrevocably.
His view was that until solicitors took matters in hand and exchanged
contracts, any conversation with a prospective purchaser was no
more than an enquiry, and that nothing became legally binding
until contracts were exchanged.   The way he put it was this :
' I don't class it as a purchase until then.'   But I am satisfied that
although the defendant may have thought that, he in fact said
nothing about it to the plaintiff.   The bargain was not made
subject to contract or in any way conditional, and indeed solicitors
were not mentioned on this occasion at all.   Judged objectively,
the parties, in my judgment, were *ad idem*, and a contract was
concluded on the terms that I have mentioned."

Nevertheless, in this case there was still no enforceable contract.   It
was contended that a sufficient memorandum to satisfy s. 40 (1) of
the L.P.A. 1925 was constituted by a letter from the defendant
containing the vital words : " I will ask [my solicitor] to get the
contract drawn up at the fixed price of £8,700 as agreed with you ".
This letter was held not to be within the principle of the *Tiverton
Estates* case, i.e., it did recognise rather than deny the existence of
a contract.   But even so it was not sufficient, because it did not
contain all the material terms of the alleged contract—no reference
was made to an undertaking to make up the road or to payment of
the price by stages.

PAGE
35–38   A similar approach to that in the earlier cases cited had been
adopted by the Court of Appeal where the agreement was not oral.
In *Edgewater Developments Co.* v. *Bailey* (1974), 118 Sol. J. 312, after
an advertisement of six cottages for sale " one vac . . . weekly tenancy.
Gross rent £468 p.a. . . . £4,000 " a document was signed by or on
behalf of the prospective vendor and purchaser stating the sale at
that price " payable 10 per cent. deposit upon receipt of contracts,
balance of purchase price on completion (time to be set by the vendor's
solicitors) . . . " It was held that there was no binding contract,
partly because the reference to the deposit contemplated a future
contract, i.e., this reference was treated as equivalent to " subject to
contract " but also because there was no express term as to vacant
possession (but cp. *Timmins* v. *Moreland Street Property Co., Ltd.*
[1958] Ch. 110 (C.A.), cited in the main text at p. 51).

But more recently in disconcerting contrast the courts have
displayed a penchant for finding that informal agreements in writing
do constitute binding contracts notwithstanding that some future
exchange may be explicitly contemplated. In *Storer* v. *Manchester
City Council* [1974] 1 W.L.R. 1403, the defendant corporation had
written to the plaintiff council tenant that they " may be prepared
to sell the house to you at the purchase price of [£2,282] " and
the plaintiff had responded affirmatively by filling in an appropriate
form. Accordingly the town clerk wrote the crucial letter saying :

" Dear Sir,

Sale of Council House

I understand that you wish to purchase your council house
and enclose the agreement for sale. If you will sign the agreement
and return it to me I will send you the agreement signed on behalf
of the corporation in exchange . . . "

The tenant duly signed and returned the enclosed form of agreement but the corporation's part was never sent in exchange because
a change of local authority control and policy intervened. Nevertheless, the Court of Appeal held that a contract had been concluded
by the tenant's acceptance of the offer contained in the quoted
letter. Lord Denning, M.R., said (at p. 1408 B/C) that :

" The corporation put forward to the tenant a simple form
of agreement. The very object was to dispense with legal
formalities. One of the formalities—exchange of contracts—
was quite unnecessary."

The practitioner in consequence must be wary that a client's
insistence on speed and simplicity does not equally mean that he
becomes bound before exchange. Thus independently in *Bushwall
Properties, Ltd.* v. *Vortex Properties, Ltd.* [1975] 2 All E.R. 214
the written agreement in correspondence between the parties did
explicitly contemplate a further exchange of formal contracts, but
Oliver, J., nevertheless held (at pp. 223–224) that a binding contract
had already been constituted (referring to *Branca* v. *Cobarro* [1947]
K.B. 854, cited in the main text at p. 34). See the implications
of *Steadman* v. *Steadman* [1974] 3 W.L.R. 56, noted *post* against
pp. 53–54.

PAGE
38

Making of formal contract.—Recent cases have illustrated surprising difficulties in the common practice by which contracts for the sale of land are made. In *Harrison* v. *Battye* [1975] 1 W.L.R. 58 (C.A.) the purchaser's solicitors posted the part of the contract signed by the purchaser together with a cheque for the deposit (agreed at £100) ; the vendor's solicitors wrote a letter in reply : " We enclose part contract signed by our client to complete the exchange and we confirm that your draft transfer is approved . . . " etc ; unhappily they actually enclosed the part signed by the purchaser instead of that signed by the vendor ; subsequently the vendor declined to proceed. At first instance ([1974] 2 All E.R. 1201) Blackett-Ord, V.-C., held that the vendor was entitled to resile on the ground that the parties had contemplated a contract by exchange and exchange only and this had not occurred—neither intention to exchange nor the statement in the vendor's solicitors' letter sufficed instead (also rejected was a claim that the solicitors had become trustees of the vendor's part of the contract obliged to deliver it up to the purchaser). However, the Court of Appeal did not accept this ground. Lord Denning, M.R., stated (at p. 60D) that the " clerical error . . . would have been overlooked " and Sir Eric Sachs recorded (at p. 61B) that he was " much impressed with the view that . . . there was communicated to the purchaser an unequivocal appropriation to him of the counterpart signed by the vendor ; that accordingly as between the vendor and the purchaser the latter became entitled to possession of that document, and that accordingly an effective exchange of contract and documents occurred . . . " Although it was thus indicated that there could be exchange without actual exchange, this was not decided, for the vendor was saved by another mistake of his solicitors, namely forgetting to amend his part of the contract to show the agreed deposit of £100 instead of £825. Therefore the appeal was dismissed on the ground that since the vendor's and the purchaser's parts were not in identical terms there could not be a concluded contract (*semble* the evidence was insufficient for the remedy of rectification).

This last ground of decision was seen similarly in *Earl* v. *Mawson* (1974), 232 E.G. 1315 (C.A.), where the purchaser had signed the top copy and the vendor a carbon copy of a typed contract for sale but with the vital variance that the purchaser had initialled certain obvious additions whilst the vendor had not. It was found that the additions had not been made when the vendor signed and held that he could not be bound by them unless he initialled them. " Although the documents were formally exchanged, therefore, they did not correspond as verified documents and there was no contract between the parties " (*per* Lord Denning, M.R., at p. 1317). Also rejected was a contention that the addition was within the authority, ostensible or implied, of the solicitors acting (one firm for both parties ; cp. text pp. 3–4).

However, uninitialled additions after signature seem not necessarily to avoid a concluded contract : the insertion of material dates into blanks has been treated by the Court of Appeal as " an administrative tidying up to be done, if at all, at the solicitors'

38 convenience " and as not affecting the contract : see *per* Russell, L.J., in *Smith* v. *Mansi* [1963] 1 W.L.R. 26, at p. 37, approved by Lord Denning, M.R., in *Storer* v. *Manchester City Council* [1974] 1 W.L.R. 1403, at p. 1408. Further, it is considered that in *Harrison* v. *Battye, ante,* and *Earl* v. *Mawson, ante,* the courts may not have distinguished sufficiently clearly between the formation of the contract by exchange or otherwise and the evidence of a contract within s. 40 (1) of the Law of Property Act, 1925 (see especially as to uninitialled alterations *New Hart Builders, Ltd.* v. *Brindley* [1975] 2 W.L.R. 595, noted against pp. 45–46).

Reference should also be made here to *Beck* v. *Box* (1973), 231 E.G. 1295, where an unqualified agent had prepared a form of contract for sale between two married couples ; Mr. and Mrs. *V* had signed the top copy and only Mrs. *P* the carbon copy when Mr. *V* resiled by destroying the top copy. Goulding, J., held that " as no physical exchange was possible [i.e., because one agent acted for both sides : see *Smith* v. *Mansi* [1963] 1 W.L.R. 26 (C.A.), cited in main text on p. 38] . . . none of the parties would be bound until one or other part of the contract bore on the face of it the signature of all those concerned, all four individuals." Expressly not decided was the sufficiency of a signature by Mrs. *P* on behalf of herself and her husband, but the lack of any such purported authority to sign on his behalf was apparently fatal. Compare *Fountain Forestry, Ltd.* v. *Edwards* [1974] 2 W.L.R. 767, noted against p. 32.

Holwell Securities, Ltd. v. *Hughes,* cited in the main text at p. 38, has been affirmed on appeal : [1974] 1 W.L.R. 155 (C.A.).

40 *" No action may be brought."*—It appears that an oral contract can be relied on as a defence notwithstanding the provisions of s. 40 (1) of the Law of Property Act, 1925 : *Steadman* v. *Steadman* [1974] 3 W.L.R. 56 (H.L.) (see *per* Viscount Dilhorne at p. 70c, also *per* Edmund Davies, L.J., at [1974] Q.B. 161, 167E) ; but cp. *Thompson's Trustee in Bankruptcy* v. *Heaton* [1974] 1 W.L.R. 605, where such reliance did not succeed. It has also been held that an oral agreement for sale between joint tenants, although unenforceable, may effect a severance of their beneficial joint tenancy (*Burgess* v. *Rawnsley* [1975] 3 W.L.R. 99 (C.A.)).

40 *" any interest in land ".*—In *Steadman* v. *Steadman* [1974] 3 W.L.R. 56 (H.L.) an oral agreement compromising various claims and legal proceedings between spouses included as one term only that the wife should transfer to the husband her interest in the jointly owned matrimonial home for £1,500 ; later the wife refused to transfer and relied on s. 40 (1) of the Law of Property Act, 1925. The Court of Appeal held and the House of Lords accepted without argument that this compromise agreement was a contract for the sale of an interest in land within that section (following *Cooper* v. *Critchley* [1955] Ch. 431 (C.A.), cited in the main text). Accordingly, to be enforced, it required either evidence in writing or an act of part performance (see further the note against pp. 53–54).

PAGE

40
contd.

Similarly in *Liddell* v. *Hopkinson* (1974), 233 E.G. 512, a husband's agreement to pay his divorced wife two-thirds of the proceeds of sale of a house if she vacated it and got married was held to be an oral contract for the disposition of an interest in land within the ambit of s. 40 (1) of the Law of Property Act, 1925 (again see further the notes against pp. 53–54 as to part performance).

See also *Burgess* v. *Rawnsley* [1975] 3 W.L.R. 99 (C.A.) noted above.

42

Penultimate paragraph and

43

Second and fourth paragraphs.—The decisions in *Law* v. *Jones* and *Tiverton Estates, Ltd.* v. *Wearwell, Ltd.* have now been reported at [1974] Ch. 112 and [1975] Ch. 146 respectively.   See also *Tweddell* v. *Henderson* [1975] 2 All E.R. 1096, noted against pp. 35–38.

45–46

Signature of memorandum.—Section 40 (1) of the Law of Property Act, 1925, does not require both parties' signatures but only that of " the party to be charged ", i.e., the defendant.   Accordingly one party is enabled to take a memorandum signed by the other only (perhaps as an anti-gazumping device) with the confidence that that other party would be bound and he himself would not be bound.   This was confirmed, although criticised as " distasteful to one's ideas of fairness ", by Pennycuick, V.-C., in *Farrell* v. *Green* (1974), 232 E.G. 587.

Where a contract is reduced to writing and signed any alterations thereto subsequently added and agreed by the parties have been held to have the consequence that there will be no memorandum satisfying s. 40 (1) of the Law of Property Act, 1925, in the absence, in effect, of the customary initialling (*New Hart Builders, Ltd.* v. *Brindley* [1975] 2 W.L.R. 595).   Distinguish the position where the signed document is altered in order to correct a mistake in the written statement of an existing contract (*Bluck* v. *Gompertz* (1852), 7 Exch. 862) or when the signed document is altered before the parties are contractually bound at all (*Stewart* v. *Eddass* (1874), L.R. 9 C.P. 311 ; *Koenigsblatt* v. *Sweet* [1923] 2 Ch. 314).   In these cases the altered document is sufficiently authenticated by the original signature. But, illogically, where the alterations amount to a variation by consent of a concluded contract, appropriate words or gestures must be directed to the original signature to achieve the same authentication : *New Hart Builders, Ltd.* v. *Brindley, ante.*   Consequently in practice due initialling of alterations should always be insisted upon ; see also *Earl* v. *Mawson* (1974), 232 E.G. 1315 (C.A.), noted against p. 38.

47

Second paragraph.—*Koenigsblatt* v. *Sweet* [1923] 2 Ch. 314 has been distinguished in *New Hart Builders, Ltd.* v. *Brindley* [1975] 2 W.L.R. 595, noted against pp. 45–46.

The decisions in *Law* v. *Jones* and *Tiverton Estates, Ltd.* v. *Wearwell, Ltd.* have been reported at [1974] Ch. 112 and [1975] Ch. 146 respectively.

Second paragraph.—The *obiter* view has been stated that in a case—

" where there was continued discussion and where vacant possession on completion formed the basis of the contract, it was immaterial whether or not it was expressed as being a term of the contract, and whether it was so expressed or not it need not be included in the memorandum, provided that the arrangement as to vacant possession that formed the basis of the contract was identical with the terms which the law would imply ":

per Pennycuick ,V.-C., in *Farrell* v. *Green* (1974), 232 E.G. 587. Thus terms which are expressly agreed between the parties but which happen to correspond with implied terms also need not be contained in the memorandum. Unfortunately, the learned vice-chancellor went on to express other views which were contrary to the Court of Appeal decision in *Timmins* v. *Moreland Street Property Co., Ltd.* [1958] Ch. 110, cited in the main text (which decision was similarly overlooked in *Edgewater Development Co.* v. *Bailey* (1974), 118 Sol. J. 312 (C.A.)).

53–54 What acts amount to part performance.—Somewhat surprising developments have occurred as to the nature of acts which may be relied on within this doctrine. In *Steadman* v. *Steadman* [1974] 3 W.L.R. 56 (the essential facts of which were outlined in the note against p. 40) the House of Lords re-examined the question at great length and held that mere payment of a sum of money in the circumstances of the case amounted to a sufficient act of part performance so that the contract was enforceable despite the lack of writing (the husband had paid £100 to the wife as arrears of maintenance under the compromise agreement). Further, the majority of the law lords severally indicated that, in the ordinary circumstances of a contract for the sale of land, a sufficient such act could be found in the fact of the purchaser instructing solicitors to prepare and submit a draft conveyance or transfer. In consequence it appears that an oral contract for sale can readily and unilaterally be rendered enforceable by the purchaser (see also a note at *Conveyancer N.S.* (1974), vol. 38, pp. 388–391). There are suggestions seemingly both illogical and impractical, that payment of a deposit or tender of the purchase money would suffice for the doctrine only if the vendor was unable to make repayment (see *per* Lord Salmon at [1974] 3 W.L.R., p. 88 ; also *per* Lord Reid at *ibid.*, p. 60). On the vendor's side, it is arguable that he could rely on the unilateral act of (part) performance constituted by actually executing a deed of conveyance or transfer and subsequently suing for the price (see *Conveyancer, loc. cit.*, where the practical difficulties are dealt with).

Reference may also be made to *Liddell* v. *Hopkinson* (1974), 233 E.G. 512 (also noted against p. 40), where Sebag Shaw, J., held that the fact of the wife leaving the former matrimonial home to enable sale by the husband was " quite clearly referable to a contract " so that his oral agreement to pay a share of the proceeds to her was enforceable.

PAGE
53–54
contd.

In contrast, no sufficient act of part performance was found in *New Hart Builders, Ltd.* v. *Brindley* [1975] 2 W.L.R. 595, where the potential purchaser following exercise of an option relied on planning applications—" lengthy, troublesome and expensive "—made and prosecuted until planning permission was obtained. Goulding, J., first doubted without deciding whether the doctrine was applicable at all to what was an unexercised option to purchase but held anyway that such planning activities did not prove the existence of any contract.

61

Payment of deposit.—Where there is an express term for payment of a deposit but the purchaser fails to comply there is now authority for the proposition that in general such payment constitutes a condition precedent to a binding contract : *Myton, Ltd.* v. *Schwab Morris* [1974] 1 W.L.R. 331 (where the purchaser's cheque was not met). However, in that case, Goulding, J., also held in the alternative that non-payment merely entitled the vendor to rescind for breach of a fundamental term (see also *Pollway, Ltd.* v. *Abdullah* [1974] 1 W.L.R. 494 (C.A.), indirectly supporting this view). Practitioners will appreciate that the consequences of these alternative positions are disconcertingly different : in substance, with the former the purchaser has the choice of avoiding the contract by withholding payment whilst with the latter it is for the vendor to choose whether or not to enforce the contract. The better practice may be to insist upon payment of a deposit by banker's draft on exchange of contracts. Reference may also be made to *Edgewater Developments, Ltd.* v. *Bailey* (1974), 118 Sol. J. 312 (C.A.), where, in effect, a provision for payment of a deposit was taken to indicate that no contract had yet been concluded.

61

Penultimate paragraph and

62

Last paragraph.—In *Sorrell* v. *Finch* (1975), 119 Sol. J. 475, a majority of the Court of Appeal (Lord Denning, M.R., dissenting) held that where an estate agent received a deposit from a prospective purchaser as stakeholder, the prospective vendor will be liable to repay it if the agent defaults, following *Burt* v. *Claude Cousins & Co., Ltd.* [1971] 2 Q.B. 426 and *Barrington* v. *Lee* [1972] 1 Q.B. 326, cited in the main text.

63

Payment of price by instalments.—A more conservative view expressed by Romer, L.J., in *Stockloser* v. *Johnson* was preferred by Oliver, J., in *Windsor Securities, Ltd.* v. *Loreldal, Ltd., and Lester* (1975), *The Times*, 10th September, namely that there could be no relief against forfeiture of instalments in the absence of fraud or sharp practice. However, this recent case actually concerned forfeiture of a deposit in a fairly ordinary contract for the sale of land where the purchaser had failed to comply with a notice to complete ; it was held that there was nothing in the facts to show that the forfeiture was unreasonable or in the nature of a penalty.

In *Starside Properties, Ltd.* v. *Mustapha* [1974] 1 W.L.R. 816 there was, in effect, a contract for the sale of a house at £5,590 with

PAGE
63

provision for payment of a deposit of £1,250 by instalments (£350 down and £16 per month) whilst the purchaser was in possession and the vendor was entitled to rescission and forfeiture on fourteen days' arrears. The Court of Appeal agreed that this was a penal provision to be relieved against. However, the purchaser was not seeking recovery of instalments paid, but only asking for time to pay the balance of the purchase price and it was merely held that the court had jurisdiction to give further time. See a full case note by Brenda Hoggett in *Modern Law Review*, vol. 37, pp. 705–709. It appears that many such instalment purchases will be regulated agreements within the meaning of the Consumer Credit Act, 1974, and therefore subject to judicial discretion in enforcement (s. 92 (2) thereof; see J. E. Adams in *Conveyancer N.S.* (1975), vol. 39, pp. 112–113).

Reference may also be made to *Lakshmijit* v. *Sherani* [1974] 2 W.L.R. 232 (P.C.), where a contract for sale made in 1948 provided for the price (£5,640) to be paid by instalments (£30 quarterly) and on default by the purchaser (who was in possession) the vendor had the option of either enforcing immediate full payment or rescinding and re-entering. The purchaser defaulted in 1952 and in 1967 the vendor rescinded and claimed possession. It was decided that the vendor was not statute-barred because his right to possession only accrued on exercise of the option to enforce or rescind. The logical consequence is that if he never exercised the option he would never be statute-barred and there could never be title in the purchaser. In the meantime, might there be a strict settlement within s. 1 (1) (ii) (*b*) of the Settled Land Act, 1925, or does the saving provision of s. 7 (1) of the Law of Property Act, 1925 (as amended) apply ? (See main text at p. 669 for these provisions.)

70 **Collateral contract.**—In *Esso Petroleum Co., Ltd.* v. *Mardon* [1975] 2 W.L.R. 147 Lawson, J., considered whether a statement as to the throughput potential of a petrol filling station could be properly treated as a warranty collateral to a tenancy agreement of the station. He held (at pp. 150–151) :

" In my judgment, the statement as to potential cannot properly be treated as a warranty. I think that the authorities indicate conclusively that, to constitute a warranty, a statement must, first, be intended by the maker to constitute a promise which can be described as a warranty, or, putting it into common language, it must be a statement by which the maker says : ' I guarantee that this will happen.' Secondly, to constitute a warranty a statement must be of such nature that it is susceptible in relation to its content of constituting a clear contractual obligation on the part of the maker of the statement."

He was satisfied that there was no intention to promise achievement of the forecast, the vital point being that it depended largely on factors outside the control of the owners of the station. See further, notes against pp. 90–91.

PAGE

72   *Third paragraph.—King* v. *Victor Parsons & Co.* on appeal has been reported at [1973] 1 W.L.R. 29.

72   *Penultimate paragraph.*—After the reference to *Dutton* v. *Bognor Regis U.D.C.* (now reported at [1972] 1 Q.B. 373) insert "also *Higgins* v. *Arfon B.C.* [1975] 1 W.L.R. 524, where such an action had become statute-barred ".

73   *First paragraph.*—As to s. 2 of the Defective Premises Act, 1972, see House-Building Standards (Approved Schemes, etc.) Order, 1973.

73   **Nature.**—In *Mountford* v. *Scott* [1975] 2 W.L.R. 114, further clarification has now been received from the Court of Appeal.   The facts, in effect, were that a total illiterate had granted an option for £1 to property developers to purchase his house for £10,000 ; the option was subsequently repudiated by the illiterate and then exercised by the developers whose action for specific performance was met with the defence that equity would not assist a volunteer.   In affirming an order for specific performance on rather different grounds, Russell, L.J., explained the position with unexceptionable precision as follows (at p. 116 E/F) :

> " As I have said, a valid option to purchase constitutes an offer to sell irrevocable during the period stated, and a purported withdrawal of the offer is ineffective.   When therefore the offer is accepted by the exercise of the option, a contract for sale and purchase is thereupon constituted, just as if there were then constituted a perfectly ordinary contract for sale and purchase without a prior option agreement.   The court is asked to order specific performance of that contract of sale and purchase, not to order specific performance of a contract not to withdraw the offer : provided that the option be valid and for valuable consideration and duly exercised, it appears to me to be irrelevant to the question of remedy under the contract for sale and purchase that the valuable consideration can be described as a token payment : and so also if the option agreement be under seal with no payment, . . . "

Reference may also usefully be made here to *George Wimpey & Co., Ltd.* v. *I.R.C.* [1975] 1 W.L.R. 995, where the Court of Appeal affirmed a decision that an instrument granting an option (for £15,000) to purchase certain land (at a price per acre) was itself within the definition of " conveyance on sale " within the Stamp Act, 1891, ss. 54, 60, and so itself attracted *ad valorem* stamp duty.   See also *Randall* v. *Plumb* [1975] 1 W.L.R. 633 as to the liability for capital gains tax where a sum (£25,000) was deposited in consideration for the grant of an option to purchase land.   Both these cases were based on the proposition that the option granted was itself property, not just the creation of an interest in property.

75   **Protection by registration.**—See further an article " Options, Rights of Pre-Emptions [*sic*] and Priorities " by Alan Prichard in *Conveyancer N.S.* (1974), vol. 38, pp. 8–26.

75   **Exercise of option.**—*Holwell Securities, Ltd.* v. *Hughes* has been affirmed by the Court of Appeal : [1974] 1 W.L.R. 155.

78–79   In *New Hart Builders, Ltd.* v. *Brindley* [1975] 2 W.L.R. 595,
contd. Goulding, J., held that where an option agreement did not state how
it was to be exercised, s. 196 of the L.P.A. 1925 applied so that any
notice would have to be in writing ; i.e., a mere oral exercise would
be ineffective unless accepted by the grantor of the option. In that
case, a notice of exercise had been sent by registered post to the
grantor but tender of delivery had been refused on behalf of the
grantor and the letter was subsequently returned by the Post Office.
It was indicated that this did not constitute service within s. 196
because the letter had not been " left " at the place of abode within
subs. (3), but that on the facts there was sufficient service because
the person authorised to receive the grantor's letters and refusing
this one " knew or strongly suspected that the registered letter
contained a notice [of exercise] " (at p. 606D). In practice it will
obviously not be satisfactory to rely on a finding of this sort and
steps should be taken to ensure due delivery without any return.
Compare *Yates Building Co., Ltd.* v. *R. J. Pulleyn and Sons, Ltd.*
(1975), 119 Sol. J. 370 (C.A.), where the option " was exercisable by
notice in writing . . . to be sent by registered or recorded delivery "
but in fact the notice was sent and received by ordinary post : it
was held that the quoted words were not mandatory and that there
had been an effective exercise.

76   **First refusal—pre-emption**—*Final paragraph.*—In *First National
Securities, Ltd.* v. *Chiltern D.C.* [1975] 1 W.L.R. 1075, Goulding, J.,
held that a right of pre-emption imposed by a local authority as a
condition within s. 104 of the Housing Act, 1957, is an " obligation
affecting land " and therefore registrable as a Class C (iv) land
charge within L.C.A. 1972, s. 2 (1), (4). However, he based this
decision entirely on the fact that s. 104 (3) (*c*) of the 1957 Act provided
that the purchaser's successors in title should be bound ; he stated
that it was thus not necessary for him " to express any opinion on the
present state of the law relating to mere private contracts of first
refusal " (at p. 1083 A/B), although this had been argued.

78–79   **General rule.**—An illustration supporting those given in the main
text occurred in *Amalgamated Investment & Property Co., Ltd.* v.
John Walker & Sons, Ltd. (1975), *The Times*, 6th March. There a
contract for the sale of a property for £1,710,000 had been entered
into with the expectation that the purchaser would be able to
demolish a certain warehouse and erect other buildings; nothing was
said in the contract by way of description or condition about
redevelopment. While the contract was being negotiated, unknown
to either party, a decision had been taken in the Department of the
Environment to list the warehouse as a building of special archi-
tectural or historic interest ; two days after exchange of contracts
the list was signed on behalf of the Secretary of State. The purchaser
(Amalgamated) sought rescission of the contract on alternative
grounds, mistake or frustration ; both were rejected. Plowman,
V.-C., was reported as follows :—

    " On mistake, Amalgamated submitted that the subject-
matter of the contract was a property ripe for development,

PAGE
78–79
contd.
but that since at the date of the contract it had already been selected for listing, it was not such a property. Therefore there was a common mistake as to the nature of what was being bought and sold and in equity the contract was voidable.

In his lordship's judgment, the issue of mistake did not arise. The relevant event was the actual listing of the warehouse, not some preliminary step in the process of listing taken in the department which might or might not result in executive action."

Equally on frustration he followed the principle that disappointed expectations do not necessarily lead to frustrated contracts (referring to *Davis Contractors, Ltd.* v. *Fareham U.D.C.* [1956] A.C. 696 (H.L.)).

84–86
Rectification (particularly re paragraph (ii) at p. 85).—In *Riverlate Properties, Ltd.* v. *Paul* [1974] 3 W.L.R. 564 (C.A.) a lease as executed provided that the lessor should be entirely responsible for exterior and structural repairs to the buildings ; the lessor sought rectification of the lease so as to oblige the lessee to reimburse a proportion of the cost of such repairs. Rectification was refused. First, on the facts there was neither any common mistake nor any exceptional case as indicated on p. 85 of the main text. As stated in the judgment of the court (given by Russell, L.J.), at p. 570c :—

" It may be that the original conception of reformation of an instrument by rectification was based solely upon common mistake : but certainly in these days rectification may be based upon such knowledge on the part of the lessee : see, for example, *A. Roberts & Co., Ltd.* v. *Leicestershire County Council* [1961] Ch. 555. Whether there was in any particular case knowledge of the intention and mistake of the other party must be a question of fact to be decided upon the evidence. Basically it appears to us that it must be such as to involve the lessee in a degree of sharp practice."

Second, after a full consideration, it was pronounced that in a case of mere unilateral mistake (which on the facts this was) there is no principle or binding authority entitling the lessor to rescission of the lease with or without the option to the lessee to accept rectification to cure the lessor's mistake (a number of the cases cited in the main text, middle paragraph p. 85, were reviewed critically).

88
Fact.—Where the vendor of a grocery business had represented that the lease of the premises would be for a term of twenty-one years from 1970 whereas he was only able to offer twenty-one years from 1967, the purchaser obtained rescission of the contract (*Mapes* v. *Jones* (1974), 232 E.G. 717).

90–91
Damages.—In *Esso Petroleum Co., Ltd.* v. *Mardon* [1975] 2 W.L.R. 147, employees of the owner of a petrol filling station made a careless misstatement as to its throughput potential which induced entry into a tenancy agreement of the station. A claim for damages was based on three grounds : (1) misrepresentation, which failed only because the transaction occurred before the Misrepresentation Act, 1967, which has no retrospective application (s. 5)—for the future, such a claim would appear to be within s. 2 (1) of that Act ;

90–91 (2) breach of collateral agreement, which also failed for the reasons
contd. noted against p. 70 ; and (3) negligence. Lawson, J., held that
the third ground succeeded : in the circumstances of the present
case (involving financial interest on both sides) a special relationship existed giving rise to a duty of care (which on the facts had
been breached) within the rule in *Hedley Byrne & Co.* v. *Heller
and Partners, Ltd.* [1964] A.C. 465 (H.L.). He further held, after
considering the authorities, that the fact that statements are
made in a pre-contractual relationship does not preclude reliance
on the duty of care (*loc. cit.*, p. 157). Although the learned judge
observed that " I am opening the door very wide indeed and
eroding the principle of *caveat emptor* and the general principle
that contracting parties are at arm's length", it is thought that for
practical purposes in ordinary sale of land cases a remedy would be
better sought under the provisions of the Misrepresentation Act,
1967. However, in connection with special relationships, reference
may be made to *Lloyds Bank, Ltd.* v. *Bundy* [1974] 2 Lloyd's Rep. 366
(C.A.), where a legal charge and guarantee were set aside because
the chargee-bank had created, by advising on matters germane
to the wisdom of the transaction, a relationship of trust and confidence with the chargor coming within the scope of undue influence.

91 *Final paragraph.*—In *Watts* v. *Spence* [1975] 2 W.L.R. 1039, in
effect, one joint tenant contracted to sell a house without any
authority or estoppel on the part of the other joint tenant. Accordingly the purchaser's action for specific performance did not
succeed, even in respect of the one joint tenant's own beneficial
interest. As a result the question became one of a remedy in
damages for the disappointed purchaser. So far as concerns
breach of contract, the default of the one joint tenant lay in his
inability to make title and Graham, J., held that, since fraud on his
part was not alleged, the case came within the principle of *Flureau* v.
Thornhill (1776), 2 Wm. Bl. 1078, and *Bain* v. *Fothergill* (1874),
L.R. 7 H.L. 158 (main text pp. 224–225) ; i.e., the purchaser could
only recover for expenses and not for loss of bargain. The learned
judge proceeded to consider misrepresentation, starting by stating
that he was satisfied that the one joint tenant, " *by his conduct*,
clearly made a false representation to the [purchaser] that he was
the owner of the house in question and therefore able to sell to the
[purchaser] " (at p. 1046 G/H ; italics supplied). Since the representation was false to the knowledge of the one joint tenant, it
was indicated that had it been pleaded the true position would have
been that he was guilty of fraud within the definition of deceit
in *Derry* v. *Peek* (1889), 14 App. Cas. 337 (main text at p. 90).
However, it was held that damages were recoverable within s. 2 (1)
of the Misrepresentation Act, 1967, since the representation even
though not treated as fraudulent was nonetheless false and the one
joint tenant had no defence under the subsection because he neither
believed it to be true nor had any reasonable grounds for so doing
(following *Gosling* v. *Anderson* (1972), *The Times*, 16th February).
Further, such damages under the statute extended to recovering
for loss of bargain.

92   *Third paragraph.*—In *Overbrooke Estates, Ltd.* v. *Glencombe Properties, Ltd.* [1974] 1 W.L.R. 1335, at a sale of land by public auction, the auctioneer was assumed to have made an innocent misrepresentation (as to compulsory purchase prospects) and the purchaser resisted an order for specific performance because of this.

The general conditions of sale provided :—

" The vendors do not make or give and neither the auctioneers nor any person in the employment of the auctioneers has any authority to make or give any representation or warranty in relation to these properties."

Accordingly, Brightman, J., held that when the purchaser bid for the property he necessarily did so on the basis that nothing which the auctioneer said to him amounted to a representation binding the vendor, i.e., the condition had effectively limited the authority, ostensible or otherwise, of the auctioneer. He further held that s. 3 of the Misrepresentation Act, 1967, did not in any way qualify the right of a principal publicly to limit the otherwise ostensible authority of his agent ; " the section only applies to a provision which would exclude or restrict liability for a misrepresentation made by a party or his duly authorised agent, including of course an agent with ostensible authority " (p. 1342).

93   *First paragraph.*—Final sentence.—See now ss. 33–35 of the Powers of Criminal Courts Act, 1973, instead of ss. 1–5 of the Criminal Justice Act, 1972.

107–   **Effect of express representation as to title.**—For the remedies
108   in damages available to a purchaser in respect of a vendor's misrepresentation of his title, see *Watts* v. *Spence* [1975] 2 W.L.R. 1039, noted against p. 91.

117   *Penultimate line.*—*Lloyds Bank* v. *Marcan* is also reported at [1973] 1 W.L.R. 1387.

132   *First paragraph.*—For a discussion of the acceptability of a rubber stamp facsimile signature by a solicitor on an authority to inspect the register, see *Conveyancer N.S.* (1975), vol. 39, at pp. 153–156.

136–   **Times for replies and observations.**—Where the vendor's solic-
137   itors purported to reply to a requisition (as to the statutory acknowledgment re documents of title) by writing a letter which gave no answer to the particular question (also failing to reveal the lack of a valid acknowledgment re an earlier conveyance), the Court of Appeal held that there had been no " reply " at all within the meaning of The Law Society's Conditions of Sale, 1953 ed., No. 9 (4) (No. 10 (4) of the 1973 revision is in the same terms) ; accordingly time did not run against the purchaser so as to entitle the vendor to serve a notice to complete : *Pratt* v. *Betts* (1973), 27 P. & C.R. 398.

PAGE
147–
148

Proof of title by possession.—No less than four recent cases independently illustrate the reluctance of the courts to accept that a possessory title has been established ; they all turn in effect on the point that the twelve years' possession must be " adverse " (i.e., within the Limitation Act, 1939, ss. 5 (1), 10 (1)), and in none of them was this requirement found satisfied. In the present context, it follows that purchasers should not readily be persuaded to take a title depending on parol evidence of adverse possession, even though theoretically this may show a good title, whatever its length.

First chronologically, in *Smirk* v. *Lyndale Developments, Ltd.* [1974] 3 W.L.R. 91 a tenant of a house had cultivated certain land at the rear from 1955 ; that land also belonged to his landlord, who sold all the property to the defendant in 1968. Pennycuick, V.-C., held that there was nothing to rebut the presumption that the tenant occupied the land at the rear as an addition to his tenancy and not adversely to his landlord. Similarly in *Heslop* v. *Burns* [1974] 1 W.L.R. 1241 some rent-free occupiers of a house of twenty years' standing claimed that at the outset they were tenants at will so that time began to run in their favour after one year (Limitation Act, 1939, s. 9 (1)) ; the Court of Appeal, however, accepted the contention that they were let into occupation as mere licensees, i.e., their possession never became adverse. Then, in the most disturbing of the decisions, *Wallis's Cayton Bay Holiday Camp, Ltd.* v. *Shell–Mex and B.P., Ltd.* [1974] 3 W.L.R. 387, in 1961 the defendants had purchased a strip of land alongside the projected site for a main road (i.e., there was petrol station potential); previously in 1961 the plaintiffs had purchased neighbouring land and had been using the strip first for farming and then as a playground for a holiday camp, which they continued to do, the strip never being fenced off by the defendants but rather enclosed by the plaintiffs ; in 1972 the defendants wrote to the plaintiffs offering to sell the strip to them (i.e., the main road project had been abandoned), but following legal advice the plaintiffs did not reply, waited until the magic twelve years had expired and then claimed a possessory title. A majority of the Court of Appeal (Stamp, L.J., dissenting) held that the claim failed, primarily on the ground that the possession had not been " adverse " because the defendants had never had an immediate use for the strip (applying the cases cited in the final paragraph on p. 147 of the main text). It appears that the subjective construction being given to " adverse ", instead of looking to *de facto* possession, goes far towards depriving the Limitation Act, 1939, of any force in this respect (see an article by J. A. Omobola " Adverse Possession and the Intention of the True Owner " in *Conveyancer N.S.* (1974), vol. 38, p. 172 *et seq.* ; cp. also *Palfrey* v. *Palfrey* (1973), 229 E.G. 1593 (C.A.), for a seemingly dissimilar approach but in a different situation). However, Lord Denning, M.R., was greatly influenced in his judgment (in *Wallis's* case, at p. 393) by his view that the plaintiffs' deliberate failure to reply to the defendants' letter rendered their claim " contrary to equity and natural justice " (no convincing authority for this view was cited and it had not been argued : see *per* Stamp, L.J., at p. 400). Lastly reference may be made to *Higgs* v.

Nassauvian, Ltd. [1975] 2 W.L.R. 72 (P.C.), where it was held, as a
matter of principle, that acts done on part of the land in question
could establish possession of the whole land (in the case, rotational
farming) but, on the evidence, that the perfect documentary title
had not been defeated. It can only be concluded that " land
stealing " will not be an encouraged activity in the courts.

Notice given by registration in the Yorkshire Registries.—The
East Riding Registry has also now been closed for the purpose
of registering instruments, although remaining open for the purpose
of making searches until 31st March, 1976 : East Riding Deeds
Registry (Closure) Order, 1974 (S.I. 1974 No. 221).

As to the equitable remedy of " tracing " being available to a
purchaser as a consequence of the vendor's position as a trustee,
see *Lake* v. *Bayliss* [1974] 1 W.L.R. 1073, noted against p. 218.

Rent and interest under open contract.—There is now authority
suggesting that 4 per cent. per annum may no longer be regarded
as the appropriate equitable rate : see *Wallersteiner* v. *Moir*
(*No.* 2) [1975] 2 W.L.R. 389 (C.A.), where following a breach of
fiduciary obligations interest was awarded at the rate of 1 per cent.
per annum above official bank rate or minimum lending rate in
operation from time to time. See further a note in *Conveyancer
N.S.* (1975), vol. 39, at p. 309.

Deduction of tax.—The reference to F.A. 1972, s. 75 and Sched. 9,
must now be read as amended by F.A. 1974, s. 19 and Sched. 1
(see also F (No. 2) A, 1975, s. 29, continuing the £25,000 limit),
which, however, appears to call for no change in the text.

Notice to complete—Conditions of sale.—Considerable activity
has continued in the courts with regard to this important practical
procedure. The notes and references are collected here since any
attempt at precise textual amendment would appear to be
unsatisfactory.

Hooker v. *Wyle*, cited on p. 216, has been reported at [1974] 1
W.L.R. 235, and *Babacomp, Ltd.* v. *Rightside Properties, Ltd.*, also
cited on p. 216, has been affirmed on appeal at [1974] 1 All E.R. 142.

In *Clearbrook Property Holdings, Ltd.* v. *Verrier* [1974] 1 W.L.R.
243, a vendor who had served a notice to complete under the
National Conditions of Sale rescinded the contract and by motion
sought an order vacating the caution entered by the purchaser.
Templeman, J., refused the order because the purchaser alleged an
extension of the period of the notice by telephone conversation
so that the vendor had not been entitled to rescind. Thus there was
a triable issue involving incidentally the question of whether
s. 40 (1) of the L.P.A. 1925 applied to such an oral extension.

In *Rightside Properties, Ltd.* v. *Gray* [1974] 3 W.L.R. 484 the
contract for sale incorporated the Statutory Conditions of Sale
(set out in main text, pp. 67–69) and the vendor served a notice
to complete under Condition 9 thereof, which specifies " at least

PAGE
214–
217
contd.

twenty-one days' notice " ; since the notice served required completion " *within* twenty-one days from the *date hereof* " (i.e., not of service)
it was held to be short and invalid.   In consequence, Walton, J., also
held that the vendor's letter treating the contract as no longer
existing amounted to a wrongful repudiation of the contract dis-
charging the purchaser and entitling him to damages.   The drafting
of the sets of Conditions of Sale referred to on p. 216 of the text
avoids the main difficulties of this decision.   However, it should be
noticed that the learned judge (at pp. 490–491) doubted whether
a notice to complete received at a solicitor's office on a Saturday
could be regarded as then served, i.e., it would be outside today's
normal business hours.

In *Quadrangle Development and Construction Co., Ltd.* v. *Jenner*
[1974] 1 W.L.R. 68 (C.A.) a purchaser served a due notice to complete
under the National Conditions of Sale, 18th ed., No. 22, but at the
expiry of the period the purchaser was himself unable to complete;
accordingly the vendor rescinded the contract and forfeited the
deposit.   The Court of Appeal held that a notice to complete
under the special conditions making time of the essence was binding
on the giver as much as the receiver (applying *Finkielkraut* v.
Monahan [1949] 2 All E.R. 234, cited in main text at p. 215).

In *Woods* v. *Mackenzie Hill, Ltd.* [1975] 1 W.L.R. 613 a notice to
complete was served by vendors under The Law Society's General
Conditions of Sale (1973 Revision), No. 19, but it was accepted that
the notice was invalid because it purported to be given by only
two out of the three vendors.   The decision of Megarry, J., in the
case was that the ordinary remedy of specific performance after the
due date for completion was not excluded by the provisions as to
notice to complete.

In *Watney* v. *Boardley* [1975] 1 W.L.R. 857 a business tenant
had duly exercised an option to purchase the reversion which made
applicable the National Conditions of Sale ; the vendor-landlord
eventually served an effective notice to complete and sought possession ; the purchaser-tenant fell back on claiming protection under
the Landlord and Tenant Act, 1954, Pt. II (main text, p. 898
et seq.) ; the claim was unsuccessful, it being held that exercise
of the option had operated as a surrender of the tenancy within
s. 24 (2) of the 1954 Act (see further the note against p. 901).

218   BREACH OF CONTRACT—PART 1.   GENERAL RULES

Certain novel remedies have emerged going beyond those indicated
in the text and applying particularly where the breach of contract
involves a sale of the land to a third party.   First, in *Lake* v.
Bayliss [1974] 1 W.L.R. 1073 (noted against p. 197), Walton, J.,
held that a purchaser had a beneficiary's remedy *in rem* of
" tracing " the land as trust property in the trustee-vendor's
hands in its new form of money, i.e., the proceeds of sale.   It is
possible that this decision should be suspect in that the vendor's
capacity as a trustee depends on the availability of specific performance, which would seem lost on an effective sale to a *bona fide*

PAGE
218
contd.

purchaser for value of the legal estate without notice, as in the case. However, a similar " tracing " remedy was asked for in *Butler* v. *Broadhead* [1974] 3 W.L.R. 27, although in respect of a breach of the covenants for title and against the contributories of a dissolved company, and only failed because of the Companies (Winding Up) Rules, 1949. Consequently the practical question arises of when " tracing " may be a better remedy than suing for damages for the breach in the ordinary way. There appear to be at least two situations when " tracing " may be preferred : one, if the vendor has become insolvent, any trust property which can be " traced " (i.e., the proceeds of the sale in breach) would not vest in his trustee in bankruptcy ; and two, the measures of damages might be less, especially if the sale in breach was at a price substantially above the market value.

The second novel remedy is in tort. In *Esso Petroleum Co., Ltd.* v. *Kingswood Motors, Ltd.* [1974] 1 Q.B. 142, which concerned the transfer of legal title to the site of a petrol station in breach of a solus agreement for the supply of petrol, various injunctions were sought, including a mandatory injunction to re-transfer. The defence *inter alia* argued that this would contravene the policy of the legislature, as embodied in the Land Charges Acts and Land Registration Acts, that only registered interests and overriding interests should bind purchasers of land. Bridge, J., rejected this argument and granted an injunction against the transferee as a tortfeasor personally liable to undo the consequences of his tort, namely conspiracy to induce breach of contract. However, this tort requires deliberate inducement, which necessarily involves some knowledge or intentional disregard to the existence of the contract to be reached : see *Smith* v. *Morrison* [1974] 1 W.L.R. 659, at pp. 676–677, where in effect the second purchaser's lack of an ulterior motive and honest doubt about the validity of the first purchaser's claim meant that there was no tortious liability found.

Finally reference should be made to *Esso Petroleum Co., Ltd.* v. *Mardon* [1975] 1 All E.R. 203 (noted against pp. 70, 90) for the tort of negligent misstatement, and to *Watts* v. *Spence* [1975] 2 W.L.R. 1039 (noted against p. 91) for the consequences of an innocent misrepresentation as to title which led to non-performance of a contract for sale.

219–
220
PART 2.   RESCISSION OF CONTRACT

The basic principles involved in rescission have been examined and summarised at length by Megarry, J., in *Horsler* v. *Zorro* [1975] 2 W.L.R. 183. There a purchaser, after a vendor had failed to complete the sale, claimed rescission *and* damages. It was held, entirely in accordance with the position as previously understood, that following a final election for rescission a party cannot also recover damages for loss of bargain but only restitution and indemnity in respect of sums paid and expenses incurred. Practitioners should be reminded that, where there has been a repudiation of the contract by the other side, they should be careful to put their client's claim in the alternative—specific performance, damages

PAGE
219– or rescission—delaying the election between inconsistent remedies
220 until the position is clear. Also it will be appreciated that damages
contd. may be recoverable following " rescission " by virtue of provisions
in the contract to that effect (see *per* Megarry, J., at p. 191 A/B).

223– ## PART 3. DAMAGES
224
The decisions in *Wroth* v. *Tyler* and *Grant* v. *Dawkins* (foot of
p. 223) have now been reported at [1974] Ch. 30 and [1973] 1 W.L.R.
1406 respectively.

In *Horsler* v. *Zorro* [1975] 2 W.L.R. 183, Megarry, J., emphasised
that the assessment of damages as at the date of the order rather than
as at the date of the breach (i.e., as in *Wroth* v. *Tyler, ante*) depended
on the award being under the jurisdiction conferred by the Chancery
Amendment Act, 1858, which means in substitution for specific
performance. In this case it was contended that damages could be
assessed on this basis even at common law, i.e., that it was not an
inflexible rule that damages should otherwise be assessed as at the
date of the breach, but no decision on the point was made (see at
pp. 195–196).

224– **Damages awarded to purchaser.**—The suggestion made at the
226 end of the first paragraph of the main text (p. 225) has been held
sound. In *Watts* v. *Spence* [1975] 2 W.L.R. 1040 (noted against
p. 91), Graham, J., ruled that substantial damages for loss of bargain
may be recovered in respect of a false representation as to title,
whether fraudulent or innocent, the latter by virtue of the Misrepresentation Act, 1967 ; the statutory right was recognised as unaffected
by the limiting rule in *Bain* v. *Fothergill* (1874), L.R. 7 H.L. 158,
mentioned in the text. Consequently in practice it would appear
to be greatly in the interests of purchasers to obtain an express
pre-contract statement from vendors of a good title free from
incumbrances. Further, even without such an express statement,
it may well be that purchasers will often be able to rely upon a
misrepresentation by conduct to be found in the circumstances
attending the making of the contract (see *per* Graham, J., at p. 1046
G/H).

Wroth v. *Tyler*, cited on p. 225 of the main text, final and
penultimate paragraphs, has been reported at [1974] Ch. 30.

In *Strutt* v. *Whitnell* [1975] 1 W.L.R. 870, a house was conveyed on
sale to a property developer and there was a breach of the contract
in that vacant possession could not be given ; the measure of damages,
being the difference in value of the house with and without vacant
possession, had been assessed at £1,900. However, the vendor
contended that he had immediately offered to buy back the house
at the contract price so that the purchaser's damages, had he
accepted, would have been nil. The Court of Appeal held that a
purchaser was not obliged to mitigate his damages by reconveying
the property to the vendor in such a case ; he was entitled to
retain the property and pursue his remedy at law by suing for
damages for the breach.

PAGE
227–
228
Power to order repayment of deposit.—An apparently wider view than hitherto held has been taken by Megarry, J., of the scope of s. 49 (2) of the L.P.A. 1925. In *Schindler* v. *Pigault* (1975), 119 Sol. J. 273, in effect, a valid notice to complete had been served by the vendor on the purchaser but completion did not take place on the specified date because the vendor's agent had not arranged access for the sub-purchaser (completion by way of direct transfer to the sub-purchaser had been agreed by the vendor); completion on the following day was refused by the vendor, the sub-purchaser then withdrew and the purchaser was unable to complete. It was held first that this last mentioned refusal justified rescission by the purchaser (so that the deposit was returnable), for " a vendor is not entitled to take advantage of some default by the purchaser if the responsibility for that default was the vendor's." Secondly it was held that, if that were wrong, the discretion under s. 49 (2) would have been exercised to order return of the deposit, for this discretion was available " when justice required it ", and was not confined to cases where the other party's conduct had been unconscionable but " was exercisable on wider grounds, including a general consideration of the conduct of the parties, the gravity of the matters in question and the amounts at stake."

Further, in *Starside Properties, Ltd.* v. *Mustapha* [1974] 1 W.L.R. 816 (noted against p. 63), the Court of Appeal agreed with the county court judge that the particular provision for forfeiture of a deposit imposed a penalty and ought to be relieved against on that ground. The relief in question was only further time to pay the balance of the price, but the inference may be drawn that in appropriate circumstances the relief could take the form of recovery of the deposit itself. However, at present it is impossible to foresee the courts treating the usual 10 per cent. deposit provision as a penalty clause : see *Windsor Securities, Ltd.* v. *Loreldal, Ltd., and Lester* (1975), *The Times*, 10th September, noted against p. 63. Nevertheless the *Starside* case could be relied on as showing that the court has jurisdiction to give a purchaser further time after expiry of a notice to complete in an ordinary case.

228
PART 5. SPECIFIC PERFORMANCE
Cross-reference may usefully be made to *Fountain Forestry, Ltd.* v. *Edwards* [1974] 2 W.L.R. 767 (noted against p. 32) and to *Woods* v. *Mackenzie Hill, Ltd.* [1975] 1 W.L.R. 613 (noted against p. 214).

248–
249
Bankrupt's trust property.—The view indicated in the text that the legal estate will remain vested in a bankrupt who holds it on trust for another as well as himself received confirmation in *Re McCarthy* [1975] 1 W.L.R. 807 (where Goff, J., distinguished *St. Thomas's Hospital Governors* v. *Richardson* [1910] 1 K.B. 271, cited on p. 249 of the text). The case concerned the situation not infrequently encountered in practice of the legal estate in land having been vested in the person now bankrupt and another jointly for the benefit of themselves jointly or in common. Goff, J., held

(at p. 809 E/F) that the legal estate cannot pass to the trustee in bankruptcy, notwithstanding any dicta or decision to the contrary, in—

> " a case since the Law of Property Act, 1925, where a bankrupt and another held property on trust for sale, albeit the bankrupt has a beneficial interest in the proceeds, because the legal estate cannot be severed at law, and the bankruptcy cannot divest the estate of the co-trustee."

Thus in such a case it follows that a purchaser has no good reason to insist on the trustee in bankruptcy being joined as a party to the conveyance.

297 **Land Registry transfers.**—Reference should be made to *Gross* v. *French* (1974), 232 E.G. 1319, and *Crisp* v. *Mullings* (1974), 233 E.G. 511, in each of which by Land Registry transfer a house was transferred to several persons (three and two respectively) as transferees who became in consequence registered proprietors whereas only one of them had provided the purchase money. The issue in each case concerned the intention as to beneficial interests, there being no statement at all as to this in the transfer or elsewhere in writing. The result in each case, since there were no circumstances to give rise to any presumption of advancement, was essentially that there was a resulting trust for the one providing the money. However, it is thought that the judgments indicate a better practice of including a declaration of beneficial entitlement in the Land Registry transfer itself in such cases, not so as to affect subsequent purchasers but so as to clarify the position between the parties from the outset. In the first cited case, Walton, J., pointed out that the Land Registry transfer containing such a declaration would need to be executed by the one person providing the money in order effectively to create any trusts.

297–
298 **Estate duty.**—It will probably be appreciated that estate duty has been abolished and replaced by capital transfer tax in relation to deaths after 13th March, 1975 (Finance Act, 1975, s. 49 (1) ; see further the notes against p. 1171 *et seq.*).

The particular point discussed here in the text, comparing an express with a statutory trust for sale with instalment payments of duty in mind, appears now totally irrelevant for practitioners. The equivalent provision for the payment of capital transfer tax by instalments relates simply to tax " attributable to the value of— (a) land of any description, wherever situated " (Finance Act, 1975, Sched. 4, para. 13 (1) (a)). Where there is a trust for sale of any sort, the beneficial interest to the value of which tax would be attributable is not land but a share in the proceeds of sale (*Irani Finance, Ltd.* v. *Singh* [1971] Ch. 59 (C.A.)) and therefore the quoted provision for instalments would not seem to be applicable. Also the ground for any distinction in treatment for estate duty purposes between express and statutory trusts for sale lay in the saving provision in respect of the latter in s. 16 (4) of the L.P.A. 1925, which has no application to capital transfer tax.

PAGE
299–
300
Power of Joint tenants to mortgage.—In their capacity as trustees (as opposed to beneficial owners), joint tenants will have no statutory power to raise money on the security of the trust property for the purpose of acquiring additional (not substitutional) land by way of investment (*Re Suenson-Taylor's Settlement Trusts* [1974] 1 W.L.R. 1280). There was some suggestion, however, that there might be such a power where a small piece of land needed to be purchased so as to avoid material damage to the value of the existing holding (*per* Foster, J., at pp. 1283–1284).

302–
304
Severance of joint tenancy.—The manner in which a beneficial joint tenancy may be severed post–1925 has been reviewed by the Court of Appeal in *Burgess* v. *Rawnsley* [1975] 3 W.L.R. 99. A house had been conveyed to two purchasers and the conveyance contained an express declaration of trust under which they were beneficially entitled as joint tenants. It was first held by the majority that, in the absence of failure of a common purpose of both parties, the express trust would not be displaced by a resulting trust for the parties in shares according to their respective contributions (Lord Denning, M.R., took the view that where the parties contemplate different objects which both fail the position should be the same as failure of a common purpose : at p. 103 G). Secondly, it was held that the beneficial joint tenancy had been severed by an agreement between the parties for the sale of the share of one to the other. Severance was effected even though this agreement was oral and unenforceable (i.e., as not complying with s. 40 of the L.P.A. 1925) and had in fact been resiled from. In addition certain helpful if necessarily *obiter* opinions on the topic of severance were stated (see *per* Sir John Pennycuick at pp. 112–113). The third manner of severance given on p. 303, para. 7, of the text was confirmed and it was stated that the course of dealing covered only acts of the parties indicating an intention to sever even though an agreement was not reached. The method of severance by notice in writing introduced by s. 36 (2) of the L.P.A. 1925 meant that earlier dicta as to the manner of severance might not now be reliable. The statutory notice appears applicable to severance of a joint tenancy in personalty as well as in realty (i.e., the suggestion that this method would not be available after sale of the land was doubted as anomalous). Neither an uncommunicated unilateral declaration nor a mere oral notice can yet operate as a severance. The policy of the law since 1925 is to facilitate severance at the instance of either party. Reference may also be made to *Nielson-Jones* v. *Fedden* [1974] 3 W.L.R. 583, where the short decision was that as a matter of law a husband's unilateral declaration of a wish to sever the joint tenancy of the matrimonial home was ineffective but where also Walton, J., made certain wider observations which were expressly or impliedly criticised in *Burgess* v. *Rawnsley, ante.*

315
Power of corporation to hold land (penultimate paragraph of page).—In *Curragh Investments, Ltd.* v. *Cook* [1974] 1 W.L.R. 1559, the company vendor was incorporated in the Isle of Man and the purchaser contended that as it was carrying on business in England (not admitted or decided) its non-compliance with ss. 407 and 416

315
contd.

of the Companies Act, 1948 (as to delivery of documents to the registrar of companies) " struck the sale and so the covenants for title with illegality or perhaps unenforceability " (*ibid.*, p. 1563). This contention was rejected by Megarry, J.

323

Investigation of title after floating charge.—Reference should now be made to the article by J. H. Farrar, " Floating Charges and Priorities ", *Conveyancer N.S.* (1974), vol. 38, p. 315, in which is considered primarily the position of a subsequent mortgagee where the floating charge contains the common clause restricting the creation of other mortgages and charges (cp. main text, p. 322, penultimate paragraph). The conclusion is reached that ordinarily such a subsequent mortgagee will be fixed with notice or knowledge of the clause and therefore unable to claim priority.

325

First paragraph.—As to not joining a liquidator as a party to the company's conveyance, cp. *per* Templeman, J., in *Re Wyvern Developments, Ltd.* [1974] 1 W.L.R. 1097, at p. 1101.

325

Final paragraph.—See also *Curragh Investments, Ltd.* v. *Cook* [1974] 1 W.L.R. 1559, noted against p. 315, which related to registered land.

326–
328

FRIENDLY SOCIETIES

The Friendly Societies Act, 1974, replaces and consolidates the Friendly Societies Acts, 1896 to 1971. The 1974 Act was brought entirely into force by 1st April, 1975 (Friendly Societies Act, 1974 (Commencement) Order, 1975, S.I. 1975 No. 204).

Appointment of trustees.—In place of s. 25 of the 1896 Act, reference should now be made to s. 24 of the 1974 Act as to trustees. In place of s. 49 of the 1896 Act reference should now be made to s. 54 of the 1974 Act as to the vesting of property in trustees. In place of s. 50 of the 1896 Act as amended, reference should now be made to s. 58 of the 1974 Act as to the devolution of property on the death, resignation or removal of trustees.

Power to buy, sell and mortgage.—In place of s. 47 of the 1896 Act, reference should now be made to s. 53 of the 1974 Act as to the powers and provisions relating to the holding of land (the comparative reference as to investment is now to s. 46 (1) (c) of the 1974 Act, instead of to s. 44 (1) (d) of the 1896 Act).

Statutory receipts.—Section 53 of the 1896 Act has been replaced in terms recognising the 1925 legislation by s. 57 of the 1974 Act, as follows :

" *Discharge of certain mortgages*

57.—(1) Where, in the case of any mortgage or other assurance to a registered society or branch of any property, a receipt in full for all money secured thereby on that property is endorsed on or annexed to the mortgage or other assurance, being a receipt—

(a) signed by the trustees of the society or branch and countersigned by the secretary thereof ; and

PAGE
326–
328
contd.

(b) in the form set out in Schedule 4 to this Act or in any other form specified in the rules of the society or branch or any schedule thereto,

then, for the purposes of the provisions of section 115 of the Law of Property Act 1925 (reconveyance of mortgage by endorsed receipt) which are specified in subsection (2) below, that receipt shall be deemed to be a receipt which fulfils the requirements of subsection (1) of that section.

(2) The provisions of section 115 of the Law of Property Act 1925 which are referred to in subsection (1) above are—

(a) subsection (1), so far as it relates to the operation of such a receipt as is mentioned in that subsection ;

(b) if, but only if, the receipt under this section states the name of the person who pays the money, subsection (2) ;

(c) subsections (3), (6), (8), (10) and (11) ; and

(d) where consistent with the terms of the form authorised by subsection (1) (b) above which is used for the receipt, subsection (7).

(3) This section extends to England and Wales only."

The form referred to in Sched. 4 to the 1974 Act remains in identical terms to the form prescribed in Sched. 2 to the 1896 Act and set out on p. 327 of the main text.

355   *Second paragraph.*—Further reference should be made to the supplementary provisions of the Local Authorities, etc. (England) (Property, etc. : Further Provision) Order, 1974, S.I. 1974 No. 406, particularly as considered by Brian Rust Howell in " A Matter of Title—the Article 9 Certificate " (*Law Society's Gazette* (1975), vol. 72, No. 6, p. 160) and by C. A. R. Webster, "Caveat Emptor from a Local Authority " (*Conveyancer N.S.* (1975), vol. 39, November–December issue).

364   **Rights in matrimonial home.**—In *Earley* v. *Earley* (1975), *The Times*, 6th June, the Court of Appeal emphasised that, in calculating the shares of spouses in property in which they both had a beneficial interest, too much importance should not be attached to their cash payments in acquiring it ; regard should also be had to their financial commitments and burdens in respect of it (e.g., repayments of loans).

365   *Second paragraph.*—As to beneficial interests in quasi-matrimonial homes, see also *Richards* v. *Dove* [1974] 1 All E.R. 888 (where the mistress had made no relevant effort), *Tanner* v. *Tanner* (1975), 119 Sol. J. 391 (C.A.) (contractual licence inferred for mistress and children and *Eves* v. *Eves* (1975), 119 Sol. J. 394 (C.A.) (constructive trust for one-quarter share for mistress).

365–
368   *Married Women's Property Act,* 1882, *s.* 17.—In *Bothe* v. *Amos* [1975] 2 W.L.R. 838 the Court of Appeal decided that under s. 17 of the 1882 Act there was jurisdiction in the courts (i) to assess the value of property and of spouses' shares in money terms ; (ii) to

PAGE
365–
368
contd.
order a sale of the property in dispute and payment of the proceeds
to the parties in appropriate shares ; (iii) to order the transfer of
title to the property as following from the power to order sale ;
and (iv) to order one party to sell his or her share to the other for
the appropriate sum.

As to the effect of an express declaration of trusts and of the
beneficial interests (main text at p. 366), in *Leake* v. *Bruzzi* [1974]
1 W.L.R. 1528 the Court of Appeal accepted it as established
authoritatively that such a declaration would be conclusive of the
question of title in the absence of fraud or mistake. In the case,
in consequence, the parties were entitled to half shares of the
proceeds of sale *except* that the husband was given credit for mortgage
instalments paid by him after the separation (but only as to half
of the capital element thereof).

368 *Third paragraph* to

369 *Third paragraph.*—As from 1st January, 1974, ss. 4 and 5 of the
Matrimonial Proceedings and Property Act, 1970, have been replaced
and reproduced by ss. 24 and 25 of the Matrimonial Causes Act,
1973. Also s. 23 of the 1970 Act (see second paragraph, p. 369)
is now s. 39 of the 1973 Act.

In *Bothe* v. *Amos* [1975] 2 W.L.R. 838, at p. 843, the position
indicated in the main text (p. 368, third paragraph) has been confirmed by Megaw, L.J., as follows :

" As a result of legislation since *Pettitt* v. *Pettitt* was decided,
the importance of s. 17 decisions has greatly decreased. For
in most cases where there are property disputes as a result of the
breakdown of a marriage, s. 24 of the Matrimonial Causes Act,
1973, now enables the court by proceedings under that section,
it may be coupled with proceedings under s. 17 of the Act of
1882, to do the very thing which the House of Lords in *Pettitt* v.
Pettitt decided could not be done under s. 17 by itself : that is,
to make an adjustment of the property rights which exist in law,
so as to produce a fair result in relation to the situation resulting
from the breakdown of the marriage."

In *Brent* v. *Brent* [1975] Fam. 1, at p. 7, Dunn, J., did not agree
that the right of a wife to apply under s. 24 of the Matrimonial
Causes Act, 1973, for transfer of property was a proprietary right
which could be protected by a mandatory injunction ordering the
husband to leave the house. He also proceeded (*loc. cit.*) to doubt
whether " a mere tenancy from a council " could be said to be
" property " within s. 24 of the 1973 Act, but this aspect of his views
has since been decisively rejected in the Court of Appeal, at least
where there is no covenant against assignment : *Thompson* v.
Thompson [1975] 2 W.L.R. 868 (as to a council house tenancy)
and *Hale* v. *Hale* [1975] 1 W.L.R. 931 (as to a weekly contractual
tenancy).

As to the court's attitude to the statutory guidelines in s. 25 of
the 1973 Act (replacing s. 5 of the 1970 Act), see *Wachtel* v. *Wachtel*
on appeal at [1973] Fam. 72, also *Hector* v. *Hector* [1973] 1 W.L.R.

369 1122 (C.A.) and *Chamberlain* v. *Chamberlain* [1973] 1 W.L.R.
contd. 1557 (C.A.) and further *Jones* v. *Jones* [1975] 2 All E.R. 12 (C.A.)
and *Smith* v. *Smith* [1975] 2 All E.R. 19.   In addition note that the
cases cited at the top of p. 369 of the main text have now been
reported as follows : *Trippas* v. *Trippas* [1973] Fam. 134 ; *Harnett*
v. *Harnett* [1974] 1 W.L.R. 219 (C.A.) ; *Cuzner* v. *Underdown* [1974]
1 W.L.R. 641 (C.A.).

In a case concerning the procedures for enforcing an order for
sale—*Danchevsky* v. *Danchevsky* [1974] 3 W.L.R., at p. 710—Lord
Denning, M.R., observed that :

" When a wife leaves the house, the usual practice is to assess
her share in money and give her a charge on the house for it, such
charge not to be enforced except on further application to the
court, but the husband to pay interest meanwhile : see *Wachtel* v.
Wachtel [1973] Fam. 72, at p. 96.   If that had been done in the
present case all the subsequent troubles could have been avoided.
But in the present case the registrar ordered a sale of the house.
And now it appears that there has been great difficulty in getting
the order enforced."

369– **Improvements.**—The Court of Appeal has indicated that an
370 award under s. 37 of the Matrimonial Proceedings and Property
Act, 1970, will not be appropriate when the matter (i.e., the contributions made) can be considered as part of the court's more general
powers to order financial or property provisions (i.e., now under
ss. 23–25 of the Matrimonial Causes Act, 1973) : *Griffiths* v. *Griffiths*
[1974] 1 W.L.R. 1350.

Harnett v. *Harnett* (main text p. 370, second paragraph) is now
reported on appeal (as to other aspects) at [1974] 1 W.L.R. 219.

In *Re Nicholson* [1974] 1 W.L.R. 476 Pennycuick, V.-C., held that
the installation of partial central heating was without doubt
an improvement within s. 37 of the 1970 Act and continued (at
pp. 482–483) :

" It seems to me that, in principle, the proper way in which to
work out that provision is to ascertain the value of the property
at the date immediately before the making of the improvement,
and then to ascertain what addition to the value of the property
was due to that improvement.   One should then treat the share
of the party who makes the improvement as enlarged by a proportionate amount corresponding to the increase in value represented by the improvement.   That can best be illustrated by
taking simple figures.   If the property before the improvement is
worth £6,000 and the parties are entitled to it in equal shares, that
is to say, £3,000 each, and if the improvement increases the value
of the property by £1,000 then the respective shares instead of
being three-sixths and three-sixths will become four-sevenths and
three-sevenths."

He also expressed the view that s. 37 should be read as applicable
severally to each given improvement, except that a series of

PAGE

369–
370
contd.
relatively small improvements might be treated as a single improvement. See also *Samuels' Trustees* v. *Samuels* (1973), 233 E.G. 149, where Walton, J., is reported as follows (at p. 151) :

> " In his view s. 37 was applicable as between husband and wife only, and conferred no rights to an increased share of the property as between a wife and her husband's trustee in bankruptcy by reason of the matters therein referred to. The section did not in his view effect any general alteration in the law. Assume, for example that *A* and *B* (not husband and wife) were joint tenants at law of a property which they held upon trust for sale with the net proceeds belonging to the two of them as tenants in common. If *B* improved the property, he did not obtain a greater interest in the proceeds of sale, but on the usual equitable principles he would be recompensed out of the proceeds of sale for any improvements effected by him to the extent to which they had enhanced the sale price. He (his lordship) could not think that s. 37 was intended to produce the result that if the improvements had been effected by *B's* wife, and not by *B* himself, any different result would follow as between *A* and *B*. But, of course, as between *B* and *B's* wife, s. 37 would apply."

371
Fifth paragraph.—*Tarr* v. *Tarr* is now reported at [1973] A.C. 254.

373
Second paragraph.—*Watts* v. *Waller* is now reported at [1973] 1 Q.B. 153.

Third paragraph.—*Tarr* v. *Tarr* is now reported at [1973] A.C. 254.

375
Sixth paragraph.—*Watts* v. *Waller* is now reported at [1973] 1 Q.B. 153 and *Wroth* v. *Tyler* at [1974] Ch. 30.

376
Estoppel; Position of purchaser.—Some practical protection for purchasers may be deduced from the decision in *Spiro* v. *Lintern* [1973] 1 W.L.R. 1002 (C.A.), where in effect one spouse was the sole owner of a house and the other spouse contracted to sell it and the former was held estopped from denying the latter's authority to do so. Buckley, L.J., giving the judgment of the court, stated the principle in wide terms (at p. 1010) :

> " If *A*, having some right or title adverse to *B*, sees *B* in ignorance of that right or title acting in a manner inconsistent with it, which would be to *B's* disadvantage if the right or title were asserted against him thereafter, *A* is under a duty to *B* to disclose the existence of his right or title. If he stands by and allows *B* to continue in his course of action, *A* will not, if the other conditions of estoppel are satisfied, be allowed to assert his right or title against *B* . . . "

This principle appears equally applicable to spouses (or others) with equitable interests under the Matrimonial Homes Act, 1967 (or otherwise) : thus if a wife knowingly stands by whilst the husband negotiates a sale with vacant possession, she may thereafter be estopped, precluded from asserting her rights of occupation against the purchaser, although possibly not losing her rights against the husband and the proceeds of sale. See a comment directly to this effect *per* Megarry, J., in *Wroth* v. *Tyler* [1974] Ch. 30, at p. 47.

377   *Third paragraph.—Wroth* v. *Tyler* is now reported at [1974] Ch. 30.

378   *First paragraph.—Wroth* v. *Tyler* is now reported at [1974] Ch. 30.

381   *Second paragraph.—Elias* v. *Mitchell* is reported at [1972] Ch. 652.

383   **Dealing with property without representation.**—The limits of £500 referred to have been raised to £1,500 in relation to deaths or nominations after 10th August, 1975, by the Administration of Estates (Small Payments) (Increase of Limit) Order, 1975, S.I. 1975 No. 1137.

394   **General rules.**—As to the power of one of several personal representatives to bind the estate, see *Fountain Forestry, Ltd.* v. *Edwards* [1974] 2 W.L.R. 767, noted against p. 32.

394–   **Date of operation of powers.**—In *Re Crowhurst Park* [1974]
395   1 W.L.R. 583 Goulding, J., *inter alia* confirmed that an executor without a United Kingdom grant of probate was unable (i) to prove title (to a business tenancy) or (ii) effectively to exercise the power of appointing new trustees (i.e., under s. 36 of the T.A. 1925).

402   *Second paragraph.*—Where a personal representative exercises this statutory power of appropriation, he must do so at the value of the property appropriated as at the date of appropriation, not as at the death : *Re Collins* [1975] 1 W.L.R. 309, at p. 313, *per* Pennycuick, V.-C.

403   *Third paragraph.*—The date of appropriation remains the relevant date for valuation notwithstanding that the surviving spouse has a right to insist on appropriation in respect of the matrimonial home : *Re Collins* [1975] 1 W.L.R. 309.

406   **Protection against liability in respect of leasehold property.**— Reference may be made to *Youngmin* v. *Heath* [1974] 1 W.L.R. 135 (C.A.), where the tenant of a furnished room at £3 per week had died in October, 1970, and a grant of administration was not taken until May, 1972 ; the administrator gave notice to determine the tenancy in October, 1972, and the landlord claimed two years' arrears of rent. The Court of Appeal held that the landlord was entitled to recover these arrears by virtue of the implied contract to pay rent during the currency of the tenancy. The personal representative would not have been personally liable because he never entered into possession of the tenancy.

409   **Protection against claims for estate duty.**—Estate duty has been entirely abolished for deaths after 12th March, 1975, and replaced by capital transfer tax : F.A. 1975, s. 49. However, application may be made by personal representatives for similar certificates of liability and discharge under F.A. 1975, Sched. 4, para. 25.

426   *Last paragraph.—Spector* v. *Ageda* is now reported at [1973] Ch. 30.

464   *Fifth paragraph.—Capital Finance Co., Ltd.* v. *Stokes* was applied
and *Coptic, Ltd.* v. *Bailey* (reported at [1972] Ch. 446) was not
followed by Walton, J., in *Burston Finance, Ltd.* v. *Speirway, Ltd.*
[1974] 1 W.L.R. 1648, where an unsuccessful attempt was made to
rely on an unpaid vendor's lien by subrogation in lieu of a legal
charge void against a liquidator for lack of registration within s. 95
of the Companies Act, 1948.

466   **General rules as to covenants for title.**—Reference may be
made to *Curragh Investments, Ltd.* v. *Cook* [1974] 1 W.L.R. 1559,
where it was contended unsuccessfully that non-compliance by a
foreign company with certain provisions of the Companies Act, 1948,
rendered the covenants for title illegal or unenforceable, and to
Butler v. *Broadhead* [1975] Ch. 97, where the equitable remedy of
tracing was sought, again unsuccessfully, in respect of breach of the
covenants for title.   See a note in *Conveyancer N.S.* (1975), vol. 39,
pp. 4–5.

482   *Second paragraph.—Grigsby* v. *Melville* is now reported at [1974]
1 W.L.R. 80 (C.A.).

Reference should also be made to *I. S. Mills (Yardley), Ltd.* v.
Curdworth Investments, Ltd. (1975), 235 E.G. 127 (C.A.), where a
parcels clause in a lease was construed by reference to the surrounding
circumstances so as to include a storeroom at the rear of a shop and
a plan referred to which excluded it was disregarded as contradictory.

485   **Maps or plans as evidence of boundaries, etc.**—In *Kent County
Council* v. *Loughlin* (1975), *The Times,* 25th March, the Court of
Appeal regarded as important a tithe map of 1846 on the question
of the existence of a road at a specific place at its date.

494   *First paragraph, last line.—Grigsby* v. *Melville* is now reported
at [1974] 1 W.L.R. 80 (C.A.).

494   *Penultimate paragraph.—*In *St. Edmundsbury and Ipswich Diocesan
Board of Finance* v. *Clark (No.* 2) [1975] 1 W.L.R. 468 the Court
of Appeal disapproved of the cited decision in *Cordell* v. *Second
Clanfield Properties, Ltd.* as to the consequences of s. 65 (1) of the
L.P.A. 1925.   The rule remains as before 1926 that a reservation
of a right must, in case of doubt, be construed against the purchaser
as being the re-grantor.

508   *Second paragraph.—Grigsby* v. *Melville* is now reported at [1974]
1 W.L.R. 80 (C.A.).

519   *Third paragraph.—Harris* v. *Flower* was applied by Graham, J.,
in *Bracewell* v. *Appleby* [1975] 2 W.L.R. 282, where the owner of a
dominant tenement with a right of way appurtenant " of the fullest
description " bought an adjoining plot of land and built a house on it ;
the quoted words did not confer such an extended right of way as
if there were a public highway and the dominant owner was not
entitled to extend the grant of an easement to adjoining land
(damages in lieu of an injunction were awarded ; cp. *Wrotham Park
Estate Co., Ltd.* v. *Parkside Homes, Ltd.* [1974] 1 W.L.R. 798, noted
against p. 577).

Principles governing the enforceability of covenants.—See now the 4th ed. of Megarry and Wade, Law of Real Property, at p. 720 *et seq.*

Last paragraph and

First paragraph.—In *Egerton* v. *Harding* [1974] 3 W.L.R. 437 the Court of Appeal found a duty to fence against a common established through evidence of immemorial usage.

Last paragraph and

First paragraph.—The decision in *Esso Petroleum Co., Ltd.* v. *Harper's Garage* was considered and applied by the Privy Council in relation to covenants in an underlease in *Amoco Australia Pty., Ltd.* v. *Rocca Bros. Motor Engineering Co. Pty., Ltd.* [1975] 2 W.L.R. 779.

PART 5.   CONSTRUCTION OF VARIOUS COVENANTS

In *Caldy Manor Estate, Ltd.* v. *Farrell* [1974] 1 W.L.R. 1303 the Court of Appeal considered a covenant in a conveyance that " the purchaser shall not sell the land hereby conveyed or any part thereof separately from the adjoining land of the purchaser. . . ." This was construed as intended to bind successors in title as well as the purchaser and was held not void as an unlawful restraint on alienation since breach would produce only a right to damages and would not destroy the estate granted. Among the incidental questions discussed but without any opinion being expressed was whether an injunction would have been granted to prevent breach, whether the covenant was in truth registrable within the 1925 legislation and whether it was within the principles of *Tulk* v. *Moxhay* (1848), 2 Ph. 774 (see *per* Russell, L.J., at p. 1307, giving the judgment of the court).

Covenant to submit plans before building.—See *Wrotham Park Estate Co., Ltd.* v. *Parkside Homes, Ltd.* [1974] 1 W.L.R. 798, noted against p. 577.

PART 6.   ENFORCEMENT . . . OF RESTRICTIVE COVENANTS

A recent decision indicates that builders may with virtual impunity disregard known covenants against building. In *Wrotham Park Estate Co., Ltd.* v. *Parkside Homes, Ltd.* [1974] 1 W.L.R. 798, certain land (an allotment site) was subject to a restrictive covenant not to develop it " except in strict accordance with a layout plan " to be submitted and approved ; the defendants purchased the land at auction and there was a special condition which gave particulars of the restrictive covenant, which was duly registered ; the defendants deliberately built in breach of the restrictive covenant and sold fourteen houses, insuring each purchaser up to £20,000. Brightman, J., held that the covenant bound the defendants but refused a mandatory injunction to remove the houses because it would involve " an unpardonable waste of much needed houses "

PAGE
577
contd.
(at p. 811) ; the damages awarded in lieu were not nominal notwithstanding that the plaintiffs suffered no loss of value of their land but were sums amounting to 5 per cent. of the defendants' profit calculated as a *quid pro quo* for relaxing the covenant. Note on the one hand that the plaintiffs had not sought any interim relief, when a cross-undertaking in damages would have had to be given, and on the other hand that the defendants had not applied for discharge or modification under s. 84 of the L.P.A. 1925. See also by way of comparison *Bracewell* v. *Appleby* [1975] 2 W.L.R. 282, noted against p. 519.

580 *Third paragraph.*—After the reference to *Cresswell* v. *Proctor* a reference should be added to *Jones* v. *Rhys-Jones* (1974), 234 E.G. 987 (C.A.), where a purchaser took a conveyance in 1970 subject to restrictive covenants imposed in 1961 and applied for modification in 1972 and the application was remitted to the Lands Tribunal for a decision on the merits.

591–
593 **Delivery as an escrow.**—Two recent decisions directly concern the problem in conveyancing practice considered on p. 592 of the main text. In *Kingston* v. *Ambrian Investment, Ltd.* [1975] 1 W.L.R. 161 (C.A.), the transaction arose from notices to acquire the freehold under the Leasehold Reform Act, 1967 ; there was some question about the validity of the notices served but in any case there was no land charges registration (see s. 5 (5) of the 1967 Act), so that in consequence subsequent purchasers of the reversion (i.e., the defendants) were technically not bound ; nevertheless, not appreciating this point, the defendants duly sealed an engrossed transfer (already executed by the plaintiffs) and returned it to their own solicitors ; then after much delay (largely due to the plaintiffs) the defendants refused to complete. The sole issue on appeal was upon what condition the defendants had delivered the transfer as an escrow : the defendants contended that the condition was that the plaintiffs paid the balance of the price and costs " promptly " (according to the county court judge, within seven days). The Court of Appeal rejected this and held that in all the circumstances the plaintiffs were still entitled to have the executed transfer handed over on tender of appropriate payment. However, the decision, although unanimous, involved a conflict in reasoning. First, after restating generally the law on escrows, Lord Denning, M.R., proceeded (at pp. 166–167) :

" Take the ordinary case of a written contract of sale. Let us suppose that the vendor's solicitor sends the engrossed conveyance to the vendor asking him to execute it but to leave the date blank. The vendor duly executes it by signing, sealing and delivering it. He sends it back to the solicitors, with or without a covering letter. There is a clear implication that the solicitor is not to hand over the conveyance to the purchaser except on completion, that is, except when the sums payable under the contract are paid. If completion is for some reason delayed, even for some little time, nevertheless the deed still holds good. The vendor cannot recall it so long as a reasonable time has not expired. Once the sums payable under the contract are paid

PAGE
591–
593
contd.

—or tendered—the condition is fulfilled. The solicitor can then properly hand over the conveyance in exchange for the money or a banker's draft for the amount.

Mr. Vinelott suggested that, if completion was not had promptly, then the condition was not fulfilled and the deed was not operative at all. The result of any delay, or lack of promptness, was that the solicitor had no authority to hand over the conveyance unless he got a fresh authority under seal. He quoted *Powell* v. *London and Provincial Bank* [1893] 2 Ch. 555, *per* Bowen, L.J., at p. 563, and *Windsor Refrigerator Co., Ltd.* v. *Branch Nominees, Ltd.* [1961] Ch. 88, *per* Cross, J., at p. 102, but I think that that is wrong. In such a case the solicitor for the vendor has ample authority to hand over the conveyance whenever payment is made—or tendered—of the sums payable under the contract, even though delayed for some little time. No doubt there may come a time when the delay is so unreasonable or so long that the person who has executed the escrow may be released and the solicitor would have no authority to hand over the conveyance : see *Beesly* v. *Hallwood Estates, Ltd.* [1961] Ch. 105, *per* Harman, L.J., at p. 118, and Lord Evershed, M.R., at p. 120, or the time may come when it appears that the purchaser cannot or will not pay the money. In that case, too, the escrow would be inoperative and the solicitor would have no authority to hand it over : see the instance given by Sir John Romilly, M.R., in *Phillips* v. *Edwards* (1864), 33 Beav. 440, at p. 447. Except in such or similar circumstances, however, the vendor is not released. The escrow, once executed, cannot be recalled. On payment being made—or tendered—the solicitor has authority to hand over the conveyance."

Then Buckley, L.J., said (at pp. 168–169) :—

"In my judgment, if a vendor executes a conveyance in anticipation of the completion of a sale the reasonable inference is that the vendor is satisfied that the sale will be satisfactorily completed in due course and that he executes the conveyance with the intention that it shall be handed to the purchaser or his solicitor on completion and thereupon become fully effective. In such a case, in my judgment, the reasonable inference with regard to the execution of the conveyance is that it is delivered in escrow conditionally on completion of the sale in due course. This inferred condition does not, in my opinion, import any time limit either by reference to a particular date or by a reference to a reasonable period. If for any reason the contract is never completed, the condition will not be satisfied and the conveyance will never become effective.

Such an inference would, however, of course have to give way to any sufficient contra-indications. The facts of the particular case must be considered."

Despite this seemingly substantial difference in inferred conditions —on the one hand, completion *within a reasonable time,* and on the other, completion *in due course,* Scarman, L.J. (at p. 170), simply

PAGE
591–
593
contd.
agreed with both of the judgments ; also a petition for leave to
appeal has been dismissed. However, some of the questions
arising from this case have been resolved by a later decision.

In *Glessing* v. *Green* [1975] 1 W.L.R. 863 (C.A.) the parties had
come to terms on a sale price for certain land with an option to
repurchase, but no concluded contract was ever established ;
so far as material, the vendor signed and sealed an agreed form of
conveyance, the purchaser made no payments at all and the vendor
served a notice to complete and sought vacation of the registration
of an estate contract. Sir John Pennycuick (giving the judgment
of the court) restated the position in general conveyancing practice
as to delivery in escrow and found that in the circumstances the
condition manifestly intended by the vendor was twofold : payment
of the purchase price and also execution by the purchaser, this being
necessary because of the option to repurchase (see at p. 867). Then
he stated (at p. 868c) :—

"We think it clear that where a conveyance is executed in
escrow there must be a time limit within which the implied
condition of the escrow is to be performed and that the purchaser
cannot insist on the right to perform the condition free from
any such limit."

In considering what the time-limit should be, some disapproval was
expressed of calling in aid equitable principles of imprecise application (as had been indicated in *Beesly* v. *Hallwood Estates, Ltd.*
[1961] Ch. 105, *per* Harman, L.J., at p. 118, and *per* Lord Evershed,
M.R., at p. 120). Further the approach of Buckley, L.J., was
preferred to that of Lord Denning, M.R., in the *Kingston* case, above,
as being the more exact and readily applicable for conveyancing
purposes (at p. 869). Finally a practical resource for vendors
caught in an escrow situation was outlined as follows (at p. 869 c/d) :

"Where there has been an antecedent contract and after
execution of the conveyance by the vendor the purchaser fails to
complete, and the vendor then serves notice making time of the
essence, the expiration of this notice seems plainly the appropriate
point beyond which it could not be said that the sale would be
capable of completion in due course within the meaning of the
condition. Where there has been no antecedent contract the
expiration of a comparable notice by the vendor if given should,
we think, be treated by analogy as the appropriate point."

In this case it was clear that any due or reasonable time had long
expired, but otherwise it appears a remarkable suggestion that,
where there is no binding and enforceable contract for sale (as there
was not in either the *Kingston* or the *Glessing* case) and therefore
no relevant conditions of sale, a vendor has justification for serving
a notice to complete designed to make time of the essence of a
contract. It is the more surprising in the context of this latter
decision, since such a notice to be effective depends on the test
condemned as imprecise, namely the passing of reasonable periods
(see main text at pp. 214–216). What is more, where there is no
contract, the purchaser on performance of the condition of the

PAGE
591–
593
contd.
escrow (usually payment of the price) becomes entitled to delivery of the executed conveyance or transfer, but will not enjoy any of the other contractual rights ordinarily exercised by a purchaser on or before completion (e.g., as to inspection of documents and even discharge of mortgages). Whilst there may be remedies available under the covenants for title, this is hardly satisfactory for the purchaser or his mortgagee.

595–
596
(a) **Register of land charges.**—The provisions (L.C.A. 1972, ss. 3 (1), 17 (1)) requiring registration to be in the name of the estate owner have been considered by the Court of Appeal. In *Barrett* v. *Hilton Developments, Ltd.* [1974] 3 W.L.R. 545, in effect, the vendor did not acquire any legal estate until eight days *after* his purchaser had registered an estate contract in his name ; subsequently the vendor conveyed the land to a third party, undertaking to procure vacation of the estate contract registration. It was held that there had been no valid registration, because at the date thereof the vendor was not the legal estate owner, and vacation was ordered. This decision was reached expressly despite the practical difficulties for a purchaser in knowing the name of the estate owner (i.e., " head " vendor, as it were), despite the wider definition of " estate contract " (see L.C.A. 1972, s. 2 (4) (iv), main text, p. 599) and despite the in suspense/effective argument mentioned in the main text, p. 596. In consequence, the third party was not prejudicially affected by notice of the prior contract (L.P.A. 1925, s. 199 (1) (i)), which would be void against him as a purchaser for money (L.C.A. 1972, s. 4 (6)). However, if such a third party had knowledge of the prior contract (e.g., as a result of a search revealing the invalid registration), the possibility is arguable that liability arises for the tort of inducing breach of contract, the remedy for which could be an injunction to re-convey (see *Esso Petroleum Co., Ltd.* v. *Kingswood Motors, Ltd.* [1974] 1 Q.B. 142, noted against p. 218). Also to be reckoned with is the possibility of a vendor's liability in damages being transmitted via indemnity covenants (see *Eagon* v. *Dent* [1965] 3 All E.R. 334).

It was also confirmed that for the purposes of effective registration in the name of the estate owner any legal estate suffices, not necessarily the one being sold (*per* Russell, L.J., in *Barrett* v. *Hilton Developments, Ltd.* [1974] 3 W.L.R., at p. 549D, referring to *Sharp* v. *Coates* [1949] 1 K.B. 285 (C.A.), cited in the main text at p. 600). Thus if in the *Barrett* case the vendor had been a sitting weekly tenant who had contracted to purchase and re-sell the freehold reversion, the registration by the purchaser would have been valid. In addition, it was stated that, had he been able to overcome any practical difficulties, the purchaser would have been entitled to register his estate contract in the name of the " head " vendor, as the estate owner at the time, which registration would be effective (*per* Russell, L.J., at p. 549E, and *per* Stamp, L.J., at p. 549H).

Certain other problems were indicated by the *Barrett* decision. Take a converse situation : a vendor with a legal estate contracts to sell to a purchaser, then eight days *before* the purchaser registers his estate contract the vendor conveys the legal estate to a donee.

PAGE

595–
596
contd. It follows from the *Barrett* decision that the purchaser's registration would not be valid and, although the donee would nevertheless be bound by the prior contract, any purchaser for money or money's worth from the donee should not be bound (cp. J. E. Adams in *Law Society's Gazette* (1974), vol. 71, No. 33, at p. 874). Again, take this situation chronologically : a vendor with a legal estate contracts to sell to purchaser (1) and then to purchaser (2) ; purchaser (2) obtains a clear official search ; purchaser (1) registers his estate contract against the vendor ; purchaser (2) completes within his priority period and re-sells to purchaser (3). Here purchaser (2) clearly has priority over purchaser (1) but purchaser (3) would appear to take subject to " actual notice " of the registered estate contract of purchaser (1) (see L.P.A. 1925, s. 198). It is an odd omission that there is no relevant provision in the L.P.A. 1925 or the L.C.A. 1972 designed to confer priority or protection on a successor in title such as purchaser (3), who would therefore be driven to placing reliance on equitable principles applied to the doctrine of notice but which may not be applicable to the system of registration (see *Wilkes* v. *Spooner* [1911] 2 K.B. 473).

As to the practical problems of registering land charges in the correct name precisely of the estate owner, see a note in *Conveyancer N.S.* (1975), vol. 39, at p. 6, where the risk that the use of fictitious names might constitute forgery is mentioned (citing *R.* v. *Gambling* [1974] 3 W.L.R. 559 (C.A.)). See also main text, pp. 603–604.

599–
600 (iv) *Estate contract.*—The common form proviso used in leases whereby a tenant wishing to assign should first offer to surrender (see main text, pp. 862 and 866, citing *Adler* v. *Upper Grosvenor Street Investment, Ltd.* [1957] 1 W.L.R. 227) has been held by the Court of Appeal to be an " estate contract " registrable under the L.C.A. 1972 ; i.e., if not so registered it will be void as against assignees of the lease : *Greene* v. *Church Commissioners for England* [1974] 3 W.L.R. 349.

For a consideration of the question whether a conditional contract constitutes an " estate contract ", see R. J. Smith in *Cambridge Law Journal*, 1974, pp. 211–214.

As to registering rights of pre-emption, see *First National Securities, Ltd.* v. *Chiltern D.C.* [1975] 1 W.L.R. 1075, noted against p. 76.

602 *Fifth paragraph.—Shiloh Spinners, Ltd.* v. *Harding* is now reported at [1973] A.C. 691 (H.L.).

603 *Last paragraph* and

604 *First paragraph.*—See last paragraph of note to pp. 515–516.

604–
605 **Cancellation of land charges.**—*Hooker* v. *Wyle* (p. 605, first paragraph) is now reported at [1974] 1 W.L.R. 235.

Reference should also be made to two recent cases examining the court's jurisdiction to vacate land charge registrations : *Calgary and Edmonton Land Co., Ltd.* v. *Dobinson* [1974] Ch. 102 (Megarry, J.,

PAGE

604–
605
contd.
ordered vacation) and *Norman* v. *Hardy* [1974] 1 W.L.R. 1048
(Goulding, J., made no order—the claim to a contract was not struck
out as frivolous or vexatious although unlikely to succeed).

605–
607
(b) Register of pending actions.—In *Calgary and Edmonton
Land Co., Ltd.* v. *Dobinson* [1974] Ch. 102 (which concerned proceedings by a contributory and a creditor to restrain a liquidator
from disposing of the company's land) Megarry, J., after a full
examination pronounced (at p. 107G/H) that :—

> " What is registrable as a pending land action is an action or
> proceeding which claims some proprietary right in the land, and
> not an action merely claiming that the owner should be restrained
> from exercising his power of disposition."

611–
612
Areas of Yorkshire affected.—By the East Riding Deeds Registry
(Closure) Order, 1974, the East Riding registry was also closed on
31st March, 1974, so far as relates to the registration of instruments
executed after that date ; it remained open for the registration of
instruments executed before that date and for the purpose of making
searches until 31st March, 1976 (see comment at *Conveyancer N.S.*
(1974), vol. 38, pp. 75–76).

620
Second paragraph.—An amended version of Registered Land
Practice Notes No. 32, relating to unverified copies of restrictive
covenants, has been published : see *Law Society's Gazette* (1974),
vol. 71, No. 17, p. 395.

622
Fourth paragraph.—In *Calgary and Edmonton Land Co., Ltd.*
v. *Dobinson* [1974] Ch. 102, at p. 108, Megarry, J., held that the
interest of a contributory and creditor in the land of a company in
liquidation was not a minor interest in land which could properly be
protected by a caution under the L.R.A. 1925, s. 54.

622
Last paragraph.—In *Smith* v. *Morrison* [1974] 1 W.L.R. 659,
at p. 682c, Plowman, J., held that :

> " . . . although s. 55 of the Act talks about lodging a caution,
> the protection given by the Act to a cautioner (namely a right,
> not to any priority, but to be heard in opposition to an application
> to register a dealing) applies only when the caution is entered on
> the register."

625
Searches.—*Last paragraph.*—The protection afforded by official
searches was scrutinised closely and found sufficient by Plowman, J.,
in *Smith* v. *Morrison* [1974] 1 W.L.R. 659.   There, in effect, a vendor
contracted to sell a farm with registered title to purchaser (1) for
£41,000 and then two months later contracted to sell the same land
to purchaser (2) for £42,000.   The issue was which purchaser had
priority.   This was largely dependent on two relevant facts : first,
purchaser (2) had been told in advance of the claim of purchaser (1)
but never believed it, thinking it was a " try-on " ; and second,
purchaser (2) had received clear official searches in respect of the
farm and had completed and lodged the transfer for registration
within the priority period.   On behalf of purchaser (1) it was
contended that purchaser (2) should not have priority under the

PAGE
625
contd.
L.R. (Official Searches) Rules, 1969, for two reasons: because he was not a purchaser " in good faith " and because the application was not " in order " as required by rr. 2 (2) and 5. These contentions were rejected. It was held (at p. 676) that " in good faith " only meant " acting honestly " and since purchaser (2) and his solicitor had had " no ulterior motive, but an honest doubt as to the validity of [purchaser (1)'s] claim " he was entitled to take advantage of the priority period (cp. notes to p. 218 as to the tort of inducing breach of contract). Also, after a detailed examination of the application for registration, it was held (at p. 681) that such applications need only be " substantially in order " rather than " in perfect order " and that, in any case, the acceptance of such an application by the Chief Land Registrar was conclusive of its sufficiency in point of form (referring to L.R.R. 1925, r. 322, and *Morelle, Ltd.* v. *Wakeling* [1955] 2 Q.B. 379).

633–
635
Charge or mortgage for securing money.—In *Re Wallis & Simmonds (Builders), Ltd.* [1974] 1 W.L.R. 391, a limited company had deposited the title deeds of a freehold property with a lender to secure a debt of £10,000 ; there was no memorandum or writing at all. The question was whether there was an equitable charge on the land of the company which was registrable under s. 95 of the Companies Act, 1948. The answer given by Templeman, J., was affirmative, with the result that since it was not registered it was void against the company's liquidator. The submission was rejected that in the circumstances there was not an equitable charge on land but merely a lien on the title deeds themselves. Also rejected was the submission that it was not a charge " created " by the company within s. 95 of the 1948 Act but rather a charge arising by operation of law ; the learned judge distinguished between a charge arising by *operation* of law and one arising by *presumption* of law, the latter alone being contractual and therefore created by the company. Compare *London and Cheshire Insurance Co., Ltd.* v. *Laplagrene Property Co., Ltd.* [1971] Ch. 499 (main text, p. 634), which was distinguished in the *Wallis* case and the application of which to unpaid vendor's liens, both original and assigned by subrogation, was expressly left open for argument in a higher court in *Burston Finance, Ltd.* v. *Speirway, Ltd.* [1974] 1 W.L.R. 1648, at p. 1658.

641
Application for registration.—For a discussion of the acceptability of a rubber stamp facsimile signature by a solicitor on an application for first registration, see *Conveyancer N.S.* (1975), vol. 39, at pp. 153–156.

765
Third line.—The reference should be to L.P.A. 1925, s. 25 (4) (instead of s. 25 (1)).

771 **PART 2. POWERS OF TRUSTEES FOR SALE**
The general rule is that trustees must act, i.e., exercise their powers, unanimously. Accordingly, it appears that any clause in a settlement or trust instrument authorising trustees to act by a

PAGE
771
contd. majority will be construed strictly : see *Re Butlin's Settlement Trusts* (1974), 118 Sol. J. 757, where such a clause which could have been read as a separate general power was construed as restricted to certain specified circumstances.

774   Implied power to postpone the exercise of a trust for sale.— In *Re Atkins' Will Trusts* [1974] 1 W.L.R. 761, a freehold farm had been left on trust for sale and to distribute the proceeds to certain persons " living at the date of the completion of the said sale ". Pennycuick, V.–C., held (at p. 767) that the statutory power to postpone sale was excluded, a contrary intention being found in the fact that otherwise the vesting of beneficial interests would be affected by the exercise of an administrative discretion.   He also found (*loc. cit.*) the contrary intention supported by the fact that there was an express power to postpone sale in relation to residue. In consequence, by analogy with the executors' year, the duty of the trustees was to sell the farm within one year of the trust for sale arising (it followed that the trusts would not be void for perpetuity, which was the issue in the case).

775   Refusal to sell or to exercise certain powers.—In *Re Beesley* [1975] 1 All E.R. 385, it was held that a spouse is not " any person interested " by reason only of matrimonial status so as to be able to apply for the annulment of the bankruptcy of the other spouse under s. 29 (1) of the Bankruptcy Act, 1914.   This decision was confined to the statutory provision mentioned and it is certainly arguable that where there is a trust for sale of the matrimonial home, a spouse who enjoys no beneficial entitlement at all might nevertheless be a person interested within s. 30 of the L.P.A. 1925 in view of the rights conferred by the Matrimonial Homes Act, 1967, and also perhaps because of the judicial powers conferred by s. 24 of the Matrimonial Causes Act, 1973 (noted against p. 369).

Applications by the trustee in bankruptcy of a beneficial co-owner have been before Goff, J., in *Re Turner* [1974] 1 W.L.R. 1556 and in *Re McCarthy* [1975] 1 W.L.R. 807 and he was able to follow his own earlier approach in *Re Solomon* (main text, p. 775, penultimate paragraph) by regarding the trustee in bankruptcy as " a person manifestly interested " within s. 30 of the L.P.A. 1925 (see at [1975] 1 W.L.R., p. 809G ;   *Stevens* v. *Hutchinson* was cited in argument in these latest two cases).   The substantial question in each of the cases was what order the court should think fit to make under s. 30 where the claims in effect were between creditors and spouse.   In both cases, in the circumstances, an order for sale was made, and in *Re McCarthy* the learned judge observed (at pp. 809–810) :

" The words ' as he thinks fit ' appear to me to give the court the widest possible discretion and, therefore, as a matter of law, in my judgment the section entitles the court, if it thinks fit in all the circumstances, not only to make an order for sale, but an order that possession be delivered up to the trustee in bankruptcy.   Such an order works more unfavourably towards persons in possession than the form of order in *Re Solomon, A Bankrupt* [1967] Ch. 573 because it results in their having to

PAGE
775
contd.

give up possession earlier than if they had simply been ordered to concur in a sale. On the other hand, to facilitate a sale, it may be desirable to order respondents to deliver up possession to avoid obstructing a future sale. Having respondents in possession may make it very difficult for prospective purchasers to inspect the property. However, bearing in mind that an order for possession, as opposed to an order to concur in a sale, is a more onerous order on respondents in possession of the property, such an order should not be made unless the facts before the court justify it."

776

Last paragraph.—Add a reference to *Burke* v. *Burke* [1974] 1 W.L.R. 1063.

780

Power to mortgage.—Trustees for sale have no statutory power to raise money on the security of the trust property for the purpose of acquiring additional (not substitutional) land by way of investment : *Re Suenson-Taylor's Settlement Trusts* [1974] 1 W.L.R. 1280. Such a power may be available, however, in respect of a small piece of land needed to avoid material damage to the value of the existing holding (*per* Foster, J., at *ibid.*, pp. 1283–1284).

791–
792

" *Personal representatives of the last surviving or continuing trustee* ".—An effective appointment can only be made by a personal representative who has taken a proper grant of representation since only in this way can his title to do so be proved : see *Re Crowhurst Park* [1974] 1 W.L.R. 583, *per* Goulding, J., at p. 595.

802

Agreements for leases and leases.—The principle of *Walsh* v. *Lonsdale* was applied in *Tottenham Hotspur Football & Athletic Co., Ltd.* v. *Princegrove Publishers, Ltd.* [1974] 1 W.L.R. 113, where a compromise agreement for a new lease containing contracting-out provision within s. 38 (4) of the Landlord and Tenant Act, 1954, Pt. II (see main text, p. 912) was embodied in a consent order but no formal lease was ever executed. The tenant contended that the contracting-out provision was not valid because it was not contained in the instrument specified by the court order, namely the new lease. Lawson, J., held (at p. 121) that :

" if a person goes in and occupies property as a tenant under an agreement, it is taken as if an instrument giving effect to the new tenancy on the agreed terms has been executed ".

Accordingly, in effect, the contracting-out provision operated.

803

First paragraph.—*Cornish* v. *Brook Green Laundry, Ltd.* has been followed on the point stated in lines 3 to 5 of the main text in *Rushton* v. *Smith* [1975] 2 All E.R. 905 (C.A.), where the question was whether there should be a stay of county court proceedings for a new business tenancy which would also involve a decision as to the tenant's entitlement to specific performance of an agreement for a lease.

803

Second paragraph.—See now Megarry and Wade, Real Property, 4th ed., p. 623.

PAGE
804   *Second paragraph.—Centaploy, Ltd.* v. *Matlodge, Ltd.* is now
reported at [1974] Ch. 1.

807–   **Distinction between lease and licence.**—See also *Wang* v.
808   *Wei* (1975), *The Times,* 5th July, where a professionally drawn
agreement on the face of it for management of a restaurant was
treated in the circumstances as a sham and as constituting instead
a business tenancy.

808–   **Variable rents.**—The decision in *Re Essoldo* (*Bingo*), *Ltd.'s*
809   *Underlease,* which was referred to as supporting the views given in
the first paragraph of the main text, has been overruled in *C. H.
Bailey, Ltd.* v. *Memorial Enterprises, Ltd.* [1974] 1 W.L.R. 728 (C.A.).
The present position, as unanimously adopted by the Court of
Appeal in that case, is adequately indicated by the following passage
from the judgment of Lord Denning, M.R. (at p. 732 c–e) :
> " I think that case should not be followed. It is time to get
> away from the medieval concept of rent. That appears from a
> passage in Holdsworth, A History of English Law, vol. VII
> (1900), p. 262, which was referred to by Evershed, L.J., in
> *Property Holding Co., Ltd.* v. *Clark* [1948] 1 K.B. 630, at p. 648 :
>> ' . . . in modern law, rent is not conceived of as a thing, but
>> rather as a payment which a tenant is bound by his contract
>> to make to his landlord for the use of the land '.
> The time and manner of the payment is to be ascertained accord-
> ing to the true construction of the contract, and not by reference
> to out-dated relics of medieval law.
> So I think these rent review clauses are to be construed according
> to their natural meaning. The clause in the present case says
> that the increased rent, when ascertained, ' shall be substituted
> *from* such date ', that is, from 21st September, 1969. It was,
> it is true, not ascertained until 23rd March, 1973 ; but, once
> ascertained, it is substituted *from* 21st September, 1969. It
> must be paid *from* that date. I know this means it operates
> retrospectively. But that is the plain intention of the clause.
> And effect must be given to it."

The Master of the Rolls added (*loc. cit.*) that if the delay of the
landlord in applying for a rent review actually prejudiced the tenant,
then the tenant might be able to reply on equitable estoppel to
postpone the increase, but that it should be remembered that it is
always open to the tenant himself to take steps to ascertain the
increased rent.

The decision in *Samuel Properties* (*Developments*), *Ltd.* v. *Hayek,*
referred to on p. 809, second paragraph of main text, has been
distinguished by Megarry, J., in *Kenilworth Industrial Sites, Ltd.*
v. *E. C. Little & Co., Ltd.* [1974] 1 W.L.R. 1069, affirmed at [1975]
1 W.L.R. 143 (C.A.). There the clause in issue was construed as
mere machinery for fixing the rent to be paid for subsequent periods
of the lease as distinct from an option to vary the rent otherwise
payable for the whole term ; in consequence the strict rule for
options was not applicable and the landlord's late notice did not
preclude him from requiring the determination of the new rent.

PAGE

813   *Second paragraph.*—In *Newman* v. *Dorrington Developments, Ltd.* (1975), *The Times*, 16th May, Brightman, J., treated as valid and enforceable options to renew leases using a formula for ascertaining the rent such as " the commercial yearly rack rent . . . in the open market " notwithstanding that the recoverable rent might be reduced by some form of legislative control (in the case, the Rent Act, 1968).

814   *Second paragraph.*—*Re Hopkins's Lease* has been reported *sub nom. Caerphilly Concrete Products, Ltd.* v. *Owen* at [1972] 1 W.L.R. 372.

     Centaploy, Ltd. v. *Matlodge, Ltd.* has now been reported at [1974] Ch. 1.

832   **Options to purchase.**—In *Re Nagel's Lease* [1974] 1 W.L.R. 1077, there was an option to purchase the freehold reversion exercisable during the term, in effect, at " the fair market price . . . having regard to values of property then current for comparable properties in comparable areas." The question to be decided was whether this price was to be ascertained on a vacant possession basis or subject to the lease. Templeman, J., spoke generally (at p. 1081E) as follows :

> " As I have said, if there is no guidance at all ; if all that you are told is that the tenant can purchase the reversion, then it seems to me that vacant possession does not come into it. When you find that there are express instructions as to how the purchase price is to be determined, and those instructions really do not make sense except on the basis of a sale with vacant possession, then it seems to me that the inference is that vacant possession is the criterion."

In the particular instance, he held that, as a matter of construction, it was the vacant possession value which was to be determined.

See also *Page* v. *Mallow Investment, Ltd.* (1974), 232 E.G. 1321, as to construing the time within which an option should be exercised : the reference to eighteen months " after the commencement of the term hereby granted " could not be treated as meaning " after the execution of this lease ", where the lease was granted on 8th December, 1970, for twenty-five years from 29th September, 1970.

In *Watney* v. *Boardley* [1975] 1 W.L.R. 857 there was an option to a tenant to purchase the reversion on giving not less than three months' notice and it was provided that on expiration of the notice rent ceased to be demandable, interest on the purchase money being payable thereafter until actual completion. Goulding, J., held (at p. 860D) :

> " The effect of such a clause, in my judgment, is that at the date when rent is to cease the tenancy also ceases and the former tenant who has exercised the option is thereafter in possession not as tenant but as purchaser let into possession prior to completion."

See further the notes against pp. 214–217 and 901.

PAGE
833–
835
C. NOTICES TO QUIT

Reference may be made to a note entitled " Quitting Dates " at *Conveyancer N.S.* (1974), vol. 38, pp. 312–314.

Centaploy, Ltd. v. *Matlodge, Ltd.*, cited on p. 834, is now reported at [1974] Ch. 1.

Section 16 of the Rent Act, 1957 (dealt with on p. 835, fourth paragraph, of main text) has had inserted the requirement that notice should also be in writing and contain prescribed information : Housing Act, 1974, s. 123. This amendment was brought into operation on 2nd December, 1974 (Housing Act 1974 (Commencement No. 3) Order, 1974) but without having any retrospective effect (s. 123 (2) of the 1974 Act). At the time of writing, no regulations have yet been made prescribing any particular information.

836–
837
Service of notice to quit.—Compare the decision in *New Hart Builders, Ltd.* v. *Brindley* [1975] 2 W.L.R. 595, noted against p. 75.

See also *National Westminster Bank, Ltd.* v. *Betchworth Investments, Ltd.* (1974), 232 E.G. 43, where the notice was sent to the tenant company's former registered office and this was held not to be its " last known address " since the landlord had had the address of its managing agents for some years.

839–
840
E. DISCLAIMER

See, as to disclaimer by the liquidator of a company, *Re Downer Enterprises, Ltd.* [1974] 1 W.L.R. 1460 and *Re H. H. Realisations, Ltd.* (1975), 119 Sol. J. 642.

844
Fourth paragraph.—It should be noted that covenants in leases, like restrictive covenants generally, may be affected by the common-law doctrine of restraint of trade (see main text at pp. 560–561). Thus in *Amoco Australia Pty., Ltd.* v. *Rocca Bros. Motor Engineering Co. Pty., Ltd.* [1975] 2 W.L.R. 779 an underlease of a tied garage contained covenants which were held void as in unreasonable restraint of trade ; in consequence, since these covenants were essential and not severable, the underlease was unenforceable, and also, since the underlease and head lease were parts of a single commercial transaction, the head lease too was unenforceable.

862
Fourth paragraph.—The correctness of the decision in *Adler* v. *Upper Grosvenor Street Investment, Ltd.*, was greatly doubted by Lord Denning, M.R., and Sir Eric Sachs in *Greene* v. *Church Commissioners for England* [1974] 3 W.L.R. 349, at pp. 354–355 and 357 respectively. The point was not there argued or decided but clearly for practical purposes the probability now exists that the proviso used successfully in the *Adler* case will be held to be within s. 19 (1) of the 1927 Act ; in consequence its reliability is suspect. See further as to registering such a proviso as an estate contract the notes to p. 599.

PAGE
865   *Third paragraph.*—The decisions in *Peebles* v. *Crosthwaite* and *Chaplin* v. *Smith* were distinguished in *Lam Kee Ying* v. *Lam Shes Tong* [1974] 3 W.L.R. 784 (P.C.), where tenants in partnership dissolved and formed a company and on the evidence it was found that possession in law had been parted with.

866   *Third paragraph.*—As to the reliability of the *Adler* provision, see *Greene* v. *Church Commissioners for England* [1974] 3 W.L.R. 349 (C.A.), noted against p. 862.

867   *First paragraph.*—In *Whiteminster Estates, Ltd.* v. *Hodges Menswear, Ltd.* (1974), 232 E.G. 715, it was held that a men's outfitters was entitled to refuse consent to an assignment of adjoining premises to another firm of men's outfitters in order to protect its own trade interests. Pennycuick, V.-C., is reported as follows :

" The meaning and scope of the provision in s. 19 of the Landlord and Tenant Act, 1927, that the landlord's consent to an assignment should not be unreasonably withheld had been the subject of considerable, and sometimes conflicting, comment over the years. Nowadays, however, it was clear that it was not for the court to decide whether consent should or should not be granted. The function of the court was to decide whether the landlord had acted reasonably in withholding consent, or putting it another way, to decide whether his decision was perverse."

See also *Welch* v. *Birrane* (1974), 235 E.G. 501, where Lawson, J., held that consent to assignment was reasonably withheld by a landlord on the ground of fearing the operation of the Leasehold Reform Act, 1967.

867   *Last paragraph.*—*Killick* v. *Second Covent Garden Property Co., Ltd.* is reported at [1973] 1 W.L.R. 658 (C.A.).

871   **Position in absence of covenant.**—A majority of the Court of Appeal has held that there is no implied contractual obligation on the landlord of a high-rise block of flats to keep the lifts, staircase and common parts of the building reasonably fit for use by the tenants, their families and visitors : *Liverpool City Council* v. *Irwin* (1975), *The Times*, 23rd July.

872   *Penultimate paragraph.*—In the second line, the reference should be to s. 32 (1) instead of s. 31 (1).

872   *Final paragraph* and

873   *First paragraph.*—A lease for a term of ninety years containing a provision for determination at the option of either party on the death of the landlord is not a " short " lease within s. 33 (2) of the Housing Act, 1961 (*Parker* v. *O'Connor* [1974] 1 W.L.R. 1160 (C.A.)).

Third paragraph.—The decision in *Brown* v. *Liverpool Corporation* was distinguished in *Hopwood* v. *Cannock Chase District Council* [1975] 1 All E.R. 796 (C.A.) with regard to paving slabs in a backyard which was not a means of access to the house.

PAGE

873   *Fourth paragraph.*—*O'Brien* v. *Robinson* is reported at [1973]
contd. A.C. 912.

874   *Third paragraph.*—The liability for repair of windows is examined
by Alec Samuels in a note at *Conveyancer N.S.* (1975), vol. 39,
pp. 91–93.

877   *Third paragraph.*—*Middlegate Properties, Ltd.* v. *Messimeris* is
reported at [1973] 1 W.L.R. 168.

878   **Damages for breach of lessee's covenant to repair.**—The
decision in *Jeune* v. *Queens Cross Properties, Ltd.* is now reported
at [1974] Ch. 97. After this a reference should also be made to
s. 125 of the Housing Act, 1974, which provides for residential
tenants the remedy of specific performance of a landlord's repairing
covenants. Note that the *Jeune* case was not so restricted to
tenants of dwellings and that the specific performance remedy is
still not made available to landlords for tenants' breaches of
repairing covenants (*Hill* v. *Barclay,* cited in the text, stands in this
respect). See also *Lee-Parker* v. *Izzet* [1971] 1 W.L.R. 1688, in
which Goff, J., declared that when a landlord is in breach of his
repairing covenants (i.e., notice of the breach must have been
given) a tenant who carries out the repairs himself is entitled to
deduct his proper expenditure from future rents.

888   *First paragraph.*—The decision in *Scala House and District Property
Co., Ltd.* v. *Forbes* has now been fully reported at [1974] Q.B. 575.

890   *Fifth paragraph.*—The effect of an order giving *conditional* relief
against forfeiture was considered by the Court of Appeal in *City of
Westminster Assurance Co., Ltd.* v. *Ainis* (1975), 234 E.G. 455.
Cairns, L.J., is reported as stating his view of the position as follows
(at p. 457) :

"If defendants who had obtained conditional relief declined
to perform the conditions, the order for relief fell to the ground.
In the meanwhile, until the time came for the performance of
any future conditions, the defendants, if they remained on the
premises, were there not as tenants under the lease but as tenants
at will or on sufferance. That being so, his view would be that,
subject to any particular terms of the order covering the interval
between the making of the order and compliance with the
conditions, it was the plaintiffs who were entitled to possession,
and if there was somebody in possession other than the plaintiffs
they were entitled to take proceedings to have them ejected."

(Lawton, L.J., agreed and MacKenna, J., dissented.) In the
result the majority held that the landlord was entitled to an order
for possession against squatters.

893   *Paragraph (e) of s. 146 (9) of the L.P.A. 1925.*—Reference should
be made to *Bathurst (Earl)* v. *Fine* [1974] 1 W.L.R. 905 (C.A.)
where, astonishingly, what were apparently common form covenants
against assignment, etc., and against trading, etc., were taken
"to show very clearly that the personal qualifications and suitability
of a Mr. Fine as a tenant were very much at the heart of this lease."

PAGE

893 contd. It was fundamental that he would be there himself and that he would reside there himself and keep the house in a character fitting the estate " (*per* Lord Denning, M.R., at p. 907). In consequence relief against forfeiture was withheld from a tenant whose substantial faults were that he was a foreign national banned by the Home Office from re-entering the country ; the reason for the ban was not disclosed but he was nonetheless judged not a fit person to be a tenant of the near-stately home in question.

894– 897 **Waiver of breach.**—The significance of a demand for rent was further considered in *David Blackstone, Ltd.* v. *Burnetts (West End), Ltd.* [1973] 1 W.L.R. 1487 and Swanwick, J., uttered the following helpful statements of principle (at p. 1498 and p. 1501 respectively) :

" My view, both on principle and on such persuasive authority as has been cited to me, is that an unambiguous demand for future rent in advance such as was made here does in law amount to an election and does constitute a waiver if, at the time when it is made, the landlord has sufficient knowledge of the facts to put him to his election. To my perhaps simple mind there is a fundamental inconsistency between contending that a lease has been determined and demanding rent on the basis of its future continuance."

and

" In my judgment, again without the guidance of any direct authority, the knowledge required to put a landlord to his election is knowledge of the basic facts which in law constitute a breach of covenant entitling him to forfeit the lease. Once he or his agent knows those facts an appropriate act by himself or any agent will in law effect a waiver or a forfeiture. His knowledge or ignorance of the law is, in my judgment, irrelevant. If it were not so, a vast gap would be opened in the administration of the law of landlord and tenant and a facile escape route for landlords would be provided. Indeed, if this were the position unscrupulous landlords could hardly have failed in the past to take advantage of it long before now."

This decision has been followed with approval by Lawson, J., in *Welch* v. *Birrane* (1974), 235 E.G. 501. Notice also in this connection *Richards* v. *De Freitas* (1974), 29 P. & C.R. 1, where May, J., held that a landlord is not bound to accept a tender of rent by a third party which might prejudice him.

898 **Apportionment of conditions on severance of reversion.**—As to other consequences of severance of the reversion, see *Jelley* v. *Buckman* [1974] Q.B. 488 (C.A.) (concerning Rent Acts protection), distinguished in *William Skelton & Son, Ltd.* v. *Harrison & Pinder, Ltd.* [1975] Q.B. 361.

899 *Second paragraph.*—In the last line, an error : delete " *six* " and substitute " *twelve* ".

899   *Third paragraph.*—The decisions cited as to tenancies at will, namely *Wheeler* v. *Mercer* (implication of law) and *Manfield & Sons, Ltd.* v. *Botchin* (express agreement), have been applied and approved respectively by the Court of Appeal in *Hagee, Ltd.* v. *A. B. Erikson and Larson* [1975] 3 W.L.R. 273. It was emphasised that the court would scrutinise closely any agreement described as a tenancy at will to ensure that it was not a cloak for a periodic tenancy. Subject to this, however, it was indicated that the genuine tenancy at will, likely to be found where both sides had had proper legal advice, represents a method of contracting out of Pt. II of the 1954 Act without the court's authority being necessary (cp. main text at p. 912).

900   *First paragraph.*—After the citation of the 1954 Act, s. 24 (3) (*a*), a reference should be made to *William Skelton & Son, Ltd.* v. *Harrison & Pinder, Ltd.* [1975] Q.B. 361, where a head lease ceased to be within Pt. II of the 1954 Act following severance of the reversion expectant thereon.

901   **Continuation of tenancies.**—Where a business lease is extended by virtue of the 1954 Act, s. 24 (1), a guarantor of the rent payable would not remain liable during the extension unless the guarantee makes specific provision for this : *Junction Estate, Ltd.* v. *Cope* (1974), *The Times,* 7th February.

In *Watney* v. *Boardley* [1975] 1 W.L.R. 857 (noted against pp. 214–217) the question arose of whether there was " an instrument of surrender " within s. 24 (2) of the 1954 Act (as amended by s. 4 of the L.P.A. 1969) where a tenant exercised an option to purchase. Goulding, J., said (at p. 862) :—

" In the older language of the law of landlord and tenant the surrender in consequence of the exercise of the option to purchase would properly I think be described as a surrender by operation of law. The law operates because the relation of vendor and purchaser paying interest on the purchase money is inconsistent with the continuance of a tenancy under which rent is payable. If that is not the right way of looking at the matter it may be that the surrender should be considered as taking place by virtue of clause 5 of the lease operating after service of a notice exercising the option. On neither analysis would it be right, in my judgment, to describe the notice exercising the option as ' an instrument of surrender ' : it was not directed to surrender as such, but to purchase of the reversion. It did not at the date when it was served as a notice bring about a surrender ; all it did was to produce such a state of affairs that the tenancy could not continue after the contractual completion date. Accordingly, to my mind, it would be an unjustified and strange interpretation of the term ' instrument of surrender ' to describe the notice as such an instrument in the present case."

Consequently the surrender was effective.

901   *Last paragraph* and

902   *First paragraph.*—Reference should also be made to *Lewis* v.
M.T.C. (Cars), Ltd. [1975] 1 W.L.R. 457 (C.A.), where both a tenant
and a sub-tenant were holding over after the expiry of their leases,
the former as a contractual yearly tenant and the latter under
Pt. II of the 1954 Act ; the head landlord/freeholder served a notice
on the sub-tenant terminating his sub-tenancy before the expiry
of the tenant/mesne landlord's term. It was held that s. 25 (4)
of the 1954 Act was not applicable to cases where the contractual
right of a tenant had ended and the (sub-) tenancy only continued
by force of the statute. Further it was found that, notwithstanding
payment of rent by the sub-tenant to the tenant, the creation of
a new contractual sub-tenancy was not to be inferred. Consequently, the notice could not be criticised legally.

See also *Dodson Bull Carpet Co., Ltd.* v. *City of London Corporation*
[1975] 1 W.L.R. 781, in which, *inter alia,* it was confirmed that there
is nothing in the 1954 Act authorising a landlord to serve a notice
of determination under s. 25 as to part only of the premises comprised
in the relevant tenancy (see *per* Goff, J., at p. 785H).

902   *Third paragraph.*—Reference should also be made to *Sun Alliance
and London Assurance Co., Ltd.* v. *Hayman* [1975] 1 W.L.R. 177
(C.A.), in which landlords had used a form of notice prescribed by
out-of-date regulations ; it was held valid on the basis that there
was no material difference from the current form.

904   **Application to court for new tenancy.**—Reference should be
made first to *Chiswell* v. *Griffon Land and Estates, Ltd.* [1975]
1 W.L.R. 1181 (C.A.) (where the tenant exceeded the time-limit
specified in s. 29 (2) of the 1954 Act and it was held that the landlord
had not, in consequence, been " duly notified " within that subsection, so that the tenant's application could not be entertained),
and second to *Meah* v. *Sector Properties, Ltd.* [1974] 1 W.L.R. 547
(C.A.) (where the tenant was so late with his application that his
status as a tenant under the 1954 Act, Pt. II, had ceased).

904   *Last line* and

905   *First line.*—*English Exporters (London), Ltd.* v. *Eldonwall, Ltd.*
is now reported at [1973] Ch. 415.

907   *Last paragraph.*—*Heath* v. *Drown* is now reported at [1973]
A.C. 498.

908   *First paragraph.*—In *Decca Navigator, Ltd.* v. *Greater London
Council* [1974] 1 W.L.R. 748 the Court of Appeal considered the
significance of the words " intended work " in s. 31A of the 1954
Act (inserted by s. 7 of the L.P.A. 1969). Lord Denning, M.R.,
explained (at p. 751 C/G) as follows :

" I think that in this s. 31A, as in the other parts of the Act
of 1954, the court has to look into the actual intention of the
landlord. It is sufficient if it is a fixed and settled intention
held in good faith which he is able to carry out and will doubtless
carry out if he obtains possession. If the carrying out of the
work so intended is such that it requires the whole of the holding

PAGE
**908
contd.**

to do it, then the landlord is entitled to recover possession of the whole. If the work so intended only requires part, in law he is only entitled to possession of the part, and the tenant is entitled, on proper terms, to have a tenancy of the remainder.

The county court judge put it well when he said :

'. . . the words " the intended work " in s. 31A mean the work which the landlord in fact intends to do, and leave no room for a tenant to argue, or the court to decide, that it would be in his interests, or the interests of the tenant, or the interests of the public generally, or that it would be sensible for him to achieve his purpose by doing some different work.'

In this case the evidence showed that the council *bona fide* intended to build a fire station on the land and to surround it by a drill yard of large dimensions. The work so intended would occupy the whole of the area. The judge held that in these circumstances the council was entitled to the whole. It was of no avail for Decca to argue that the council might construct an adequate fire station in a different way. I entirely agree."

(Stephenson, L.J., at p. 753, also quoted the passage from the county court judgment with approval.)

909

Last paragraph.—Insert at the beginning the shoulder heading : **Terms of new tenancy.**

Add after the citation of *Re No. 88 High Road, Kilburn* a cross-reference to pp. 904–905 as to applications for reasonable interim rents to be determined.

910

Last paragraph.—It has been confirmed that the court has no power, on an application under Pt. II of the 1954 Act, to enlarge the original holding : *G. Orlik (Meat Products), Ltd.* v. *Hastings and Thanet Building Society* (1974), *The Times,* 31st October, where the inclusion of additional rights of access over the landlord's adjoining land was sought. Query : would the result sought not be achieved anyway by virtue of the rules as to the implied grant of easements ? See main text at p. 506 *et seq.*

912

Contracting-out prohibited.—See also *Tottenham Hotspur Football & Athletic Co., Ltd.* v. *Princegrove Publishers, Ltd.* [1974] 1 W.L.R. 113, noted against p. 802, and compare *Hagee, Ltd.* v. *A. B. Erikson and Larson* [1975] 3 W.L.R. 273, noted against p. 899.

918

(1) Tenant.—It has been held that in the 1967 Act, and in particular in s. 1 (2) (*b*), the reference to a " mortgage term " means a term under a subsisting mortgage : *Re " Fairview ", Church Street, Bromyard* [1974] 1 W.L.R. 579, Megarry, J. Accordingly the tenant of a house holding the residue of a term of 200 years at a peppercorn rent created by a mortgage dated 1813 where the right of redemption had ceased on a sale in 1862 was entitled to apply for enfranchisement.

920   (2) **House.**—The Housing Act, 1974, s. 118 (which section came into force on 31st July, 1974), in effect raises the rateable value limits mentioned in the first paragraph to £1,500 in Greater London and £750 elsewhere, *unless* the tenancy was created after 18th February, 1966, when the limits are £1,000 in Greater London and £500 elsewhere (the appropriate day for determining rateable values has reference to 1st April, 1973). A landlord affected by this section has until 31st July, 1976, to apply to the Secretary of State for the Environment for retention of management powers (see p. 933 of main text). A tenant is able to achieve a notional reduction of the rateable value (for the purpose of the 1967 Act limits) on account of tenants' improvements (the procedure is set out in Sched. 8 to the 1974 Act). Also designed to prevent tenants from being penalised by their own efforts, a new formula is provided for calculating the price to enable deduction of the value of tenants' improvements where the rateable value (reduced as above) is above £1,000 in Greater London or £500 elsewhere. See note to p. 928 of main text. Reference may be made to a useful article on these new provisions, containing worked examples, by C. C. Hubbard in *Estates Gazette* (1975), vol. 234, pp. 729–737.

920   *Second paragraph.*—In the House of Lords in *Parsons* v. *Trustees of Henry Smith's Charity* on appeal at [1974] 1 W.L.R. 435 the question of the rateable value of the premises was said to be one depending on numerous difficulties and was expressly left open for further consideration (see *per* Lord Wilberforce at p. 440).

921   *First paragraph.*—The decision in *Parsons* v. *Trustees of Henry Smith's Charity* has been affirmed by the House of Lords at [1974] 1 W.L.R. 435, where the materiality of the overhang was not in issue but it was contended unsuccessfully that despite the overhang due to its proper construction there was a structurally detached house.

Contrast *Gaidowski* v. *Gonville and Caius College, Cambridge* [1975] 1 W.L.R. 1067 (C.A.), where an application for enfranchisement succeeded in respect of one of a pair of semi-detached houses notwithstanding that the tenant had also used one room in the other (the access to that room was bricked up before the application and it was not included in the application) ; the one semi, as a matter of factual commonsense, was a " house " within the 1967 Act.

921   *Second paragraph.*—The difficulties of the " let . . . with " requirement in s. 2 (3) of the 1967 Act were considered by the Court of Appeal in *Gaidowski* v. *Gonville and Caius College, Cambridge* [1975] 1 W.L.R. 1067 with regard to a strip of land used by the tenant as a garden which had eventually (via sub-letting and assignment of the mesne tenancy) become let by the lessor to the tenant. Ormrod, L.J., doubted whether the Rent Acts cases were of any assistance since the purposes of the statutes were quite different (at p. 1072H). He said that : " In my judgment, ' let with ' implies some reasonably close connection between the

PAGE

921 transactions of letting the homes and letting the strip " (at p. 1073A).
contd. Similarly Sir Gordon Willmer said : " I do not go so far as to say
that the properties must both be let as part of the same transaction.
But there must, in my view, be at least some connecting link between
the letting of the one property and the letting of the other. No
such link exists in the present case " (at p. 1074 c/d). Accordingly,
the garden strip was excluded from the enfranchisement.

922 *Last paragraph* and

923 *First paragraph.*—In *Austin* v. *Dick Richards Properties, Ltd.*
[1975] 1 W.L.R. 1033 (C.A.) the tenant under a long lease had been
granted a consecutive fifteen-year lease and had later assigned the
remainder of the second lease. It was held that the assignee could
claim in his own right to be a tenant under a long lease ; by s. 3 (2)
of the 1967 Act the second lease is deemed to be a long lease for
the benefit not only of the tenant but of anyone in whom it becomes
vested by assignment or otherwise (see *per* Mackenna, J., at
p. 1036 A/B).

924 **(4) Low rent.**—The meaning of the phrase " letting value " in
s. 4 (1) proviso of the 1967 Act was considered by the Court of
Appeal in *Gidlow-Jackson* v. *Middlegate Properties, Ltd.* [1974]
Q.B. 361. It was decided that regard had to be had to " the
existence of a statutory ceiling upon the amount of rent lawfully
exigible from the tenant by the landlord " (see *per* Roskill, L.J.,
at p. 378G) ; in other words, the " letting value " could not exceed
the maximum rent recoverable under the Rent Acts at the commencement of the tenancy. In the case, the tenancy commenced in 1953
for a twenty-eight-year term at a rent of £70 a year ; the then
standard rent of £90 a year was treated as the maximum exigible
rent by the majority of the court ; therefore, since £70 was more
than two-thirds of £90, the tenant was not entitled to enfranchisement. Compare the approach, for different purposes, in *Becker
Grossmith & Co.* v. *Canworth Group, Ltd.* [1974] 3 All E.R. 561.

928 **Price.**—Section 118 (4) of the Housing Act, 1974, as noted
against p. 920, has elaborated this formula for calculating the price
by inserting a new subsection into s. 9 of the 1967 Act, as follows :

" (1A) Notwithstanding, the foregoing subsection, the price
payable for a house and premises, the rateable value of which is
above £1,000 in Greater London and £500 elsewhere, on a conveyance under section 8 above, shall be the amount which at the
relevant time the house and premises, if sold in the open market
by a willing seller, might be expected to realise on the following
assumptions :—

(a) on the assumption that the vendor was selling for an estate
in fee simple, subject to the tenancy, but on the assumption
that this Part of this Act conferred no right to acquire
the freehold ;

**928
contd.**

    (*b*) on the assumption that at the end of the tenancy the tenant has the right to remain in possession of the house and premises under the provisions of Part I of the Landlord and Tenant Act 1954 ;

    (*c*) on the assumption that the tenant has no liability to carry out any repairs, maintenance or redecorations under the terms of the tenancy or Part I of the Landlord and Tenant Act 1954 ;

    (*d*) on the assumption that the price be diminished by the extent to which the value of the house and premises has been increased by any improvement carried out by the tenant or his predecessors in title at their own expense ;

    (*e*) on the assumption that (subject to paragraph (*a*) above) the vendor was selling subject, in respect of rent charges and other rents to which section 11 (2) below applies, to the same annual charge as the conveyance to the tenant is to be subject to, but the purchaser would otherwise be effectively exonerated until the termination of the tenancy from any liability or charge in respect of tenant's incumbrances ; and

    (*f*) on the assumption that (subject to paragraphs (*a*) and (*b*) above) the vendor was selling with and subject to the rights and burdens with and subject to which the conveyance to the tenant is to be made, and in particular with and subject to such permanent or extended rights and burdens as are to be created in order to give effect to section 10 below."

After the citation of *Official Custodian for Charities* v. *Goldridge* reference may also be made to an article by Trevor M. Aldridge in *Solicitors' Journal* (1974), vol. 118, pp. 107–108.

933   **Management scheme.**—As to landlords applying before 31st July, 1976, in consequence of the increase in rateable value limits by s. 118 of the Housing Act, 1974, see note against p. 920.

934   **B. PART I OF THE LANDLORD AND TENANT ACT, 1954**

By s. 17 of the 1954 Act, the provisions of Pt. I " shall have effect notwithstanding any agreement to the contrary : Provided that nothing in this Part of this Act shall be construed as preventing the surrender of a tenancy." In *Re Hennessey's Agreement* [1975] 2 W.L.R. 159, Plowman, V.-C., held that on the true construction of s. 17, the proviso means an actual surrender of the tenancy so that an agreement to surrender the tenancy *in futuro* was caught by the section. In the case certain option provisions were construed as such agreements to surrender and so were void by virtue of s. 17.

943   *Last paragraph.*—At the end a reference should be made to *McClinton* v. *McFall* (1974), 232 E.G. 707 (C.A.), where it was held that the tenancy was in substance of agricultural land, its

PAGE
943
contd.
main use being for pasture, grazing and haymaking, although it was also used concurrently to some extent for the business of a stud farm carried on by the tenant on neighbouring land.

944   *First paragraph.*—At the end, add : Compare *Darby* v. *Williams* (1974), 232 E.G. 579 (C.A.), where there were two separate tenancies of a furnished cottage and of abutting agricultural land and the tenancy of the former was not treated as an agricultural holding.

944   *Second paragraph.*—In *Bahamas International Trust Co., Ltd.* v. *Threadgold* [1974] 1 W.L.R. 1514 the House of Lords considered an agreement whereby a deceased tenant's son was allowed to occupy the farmhouse rent free for eleven months subject to fifty-six days' notice, was employed as caretaker at 10s per week and was allowed to retain his cows on the land for seven months. The law lords pronounced that :—

" To come within s. 2 (1) of the Agricultural Holdings Act, 1948, the licence granted under an agreement must be a ' licence to *occupy* land for use as agricultural land.' To satisfy this require- ment the right of occupation for agricultural purposes must be an exclusive right under which the grantee is entitled to prevent the grantor and any other person authorised by the grantor from making any use of the land, at any rate for agricultural purposes, during the period of the grant."

(*per* Lord Diplock, at p. 1527 G/H, with whom the others simply agreed).

It was held that the agreement in question did not constitute such a licence.

947   *Last line.*—Reference may be made to an article by J. Muir Watt about practical points arising from the 1973 regulations in *Solicitors' Journal* (1974), vol. 118, pp. 266–268.

953   *Paragraph (b).*—*Rugby Joint Water Board* v. *Foottit* is now reported at [1973] A.C. 202.

953–   *Paragraph (d).*—The courts have adopted an apparently harsh
954   approach to notices served under s. 24 (2) (*d*) of the 1948 Act.

In *Pickard* v. *Bishop* (1975), 235 E.G. 133, the notice to pay rent had named the wrong person as landlord (i.e., Mr. J. L. H. Arkwright rather than the trustees of a discretionary settlement created by him) and a majority of the Court of Appeal held it a bad notice. Lord Denning, M.R., observed (at p. 135) :

" In construing s. 24 (2) (*d*) it must be recognised that it is a provision which enables the landlord to forfeit the tenant's interest and obtain possession, to the great advantage of the landlord and great loss of the tenant. Now it is a settled rule of construction that forfeiture clauses are to be construed strictly. The party who seeks to enforce a forfeiture must comply strictly with every requirement leading to it. I would therefore construe s. 24 (2) (*d*) strictly so as to require the landlords to fulfil it to the letter."

PAGE

953– In *Wykes* v. *Davis* [1975] 2 W.L.R. 131 (C.A.) a notice to remedy
954 a number of breaches within a specified period (seven months) had
contd. been served and the tenants had completed most but not all of the
remedial work by its expiry ; it was held not a valid notice. As
Brown, L.J., shortly put it (at p. 142H) :

" Where, as here, the notice to remedy specifies a single period
for remedying a number of breaches, I agree, for the reasons
given by Buckley, L.J., that on the true construction of s. 24 (2) (*d*)
of the Act of 1948 and s. 19 (1) of the Act of 1963 that period
must be a reasonable period for remedying *all* the breaches
specified in the notice and that if the period allowed is not a
reasonable one for remedying *all* the breaches, the notice is
invalid."

Leave to appeal to the House of Lords was granted.

955 *Last paragraph* and

956 *First paragraph.*—In *Magdalen College, Oxford* v. *Heritage* [1974]
1 W.L.R. 441 (C.A.) a notice to pay rent failing to specify the
period for payment was followed by a notice to quit given by
reason of failure to comply with the earlier notice ; it was held
(1) that the tenant was precluded by art. 9 of the 1964 Order from
contesting, otherwise than by arbitration and within the time limit
provided, the validity of the notice to quit on the ground of an
objection to the notice to pay ; (2) that the notice to quit was not
invalid for failing to set out verbatim the words of s. 24 (2) (*d*) of
the 1948 Act since it indicated the reason sufficiently clearly.

See also *Mercantile and General Reinsurance Co., Ltd.* v. *Groves*
[1974] Q.B. 43 (C.A.), where a second notice to remedy breaches
was served within twelve months of the earlier notice (i.e., contrary
to s. 19 (1) (*b*) of the Agriculture (Miscellaneous Provisions) Act,
1963) ; a notice to quit based on non-compliance with the second
notice was held valid since the earlier notice had been withdrawn
with the tenant's agreement in writing.

959 **Service of notice to quit.**—In *Lord Newborough* v. *Jones* [1975]
Ch. 90 a notice to quit an agricultural holding was pushed by the
landlord under the tenant's door and the tenant claimed that it
had remained unknown beneath the linoleum for five months.
The Court of Appeal held that s. 92 (1) of the 1948 Act only required
that a notice be left at the tenant's address in a manner in which
a reasonable person would adopt in order to bring it to the tenant's
attention and that putting it under the door was such a manner
so that the service was valid.

960– D. CLAIMS FOR COMPENSATION
966

The Agriculture (Calculation of Value for Compensation) (Amendment) Regulations, 1975, prescribe revised scales of unit values
for calculating the compensation payable by landlords to tenant
farmers for short term improvements and tenant right matters

PAGE
960–
966
contd.
when agricultural tenancies come to an end on or after 7th February, 1975. The new regulations increase the amounts payable for the residual manurial value of certain fertilisers applied to the land and the unexhausted manurial value of certain feedingstuffs fed on the holding and for the settled value of hill sheep on hill land. They take account of rises in prices and costs and of the ending of the fertiliser subsidy.

970
et seq.

MORTGAGES

CONSUMER CREDIT ACT, 1974

The existing law of mortgages of land given in the text depends principally upon a peculiar amalgamation of the rules of common law, the principles of equity and the provisions of the 1925 property legislation. Now the subject is to be affected, as a related matter, by the comprehensive code for regulating the supply of cash loans or any form of financial accommodation to individuals to be established under the Consumer Credit Act, 1974. An account of these novel statutory provisions, so far as relevant, is given under the general head of Mortgages since it would be quite impractical to attempt to indicate their impact in the line-by-line noter-up manner. Further the account can only be in introductory outline in this Supplement because at the time of writing the relevant provisions have not yet been brought into actual operation and also because the operation of the Act will necessarily require a vast mass of regulations and orders through subordinate legislation which has not yet been made. For a detailed consideration, see an article by J. E. Adams entitled " Mortgages and the Consumer Credit Act, 1974 " in *Conveyancer N.S.* (1975), vol. 39, pp. 94–115. As will be seen, it is thought that the application of the new code to mortgages of land in practice will not only be limited but also call for little more than the appropriate use of standard statutory forms.

Limits and exemption.—The 1974 Act can only affect (i.e., regulate) a mortgage which constitutes a " consumer credit agreement ", which means an agreement between an individual (including a partnership or other incorporated body) and any other person whereby the latter (i.e., the creditor) provides the former (i.e., the debtor) with *credit not exceeding £5,000* (ss. 8 and 189 ; this money limit can be altered : s. 181). Here " credit " includes " a cash loan and any other form of financial accommodation " (s. 9 (1)), which appears an extremely wide definition. However, a mortgage of land within these limits may still be *exempt* from regulation under the 1974 Act if it meets both of two criteria (s. 16), the first (1) relating to the lender and the second (2) relating to the nature of the loan. The exempting provision is as follows :

" (1) This Act does not regulate a consumer credit agreement where the creditor is a local authority or building society, or a body specified, or of a description specified, in an order made by the Secretary of State, being—

(*a*) an insurance company,

PAGE
970
et seq.
contd.

(*b*) a friendly society,

(*c*) an organisation of employers or organisation of workers,

(*d*) a charity,

(*e*) a land improvement company, or

(*f*) a body corporate named or specifically referred to in any public general Act.

(2) Subsection (1) applies only where the agreement is—

(*a*) a debtor-creditor-supplier agreement financing—

    (i) the purchase of land, or

    (ii) the provision of dwellings on any land,

and secured by a land mortgage on that land ; or

(*b*) a debtor-creditor agreement secured by any land mortgage ; or

(*c*) a debtor-creditor-supplier agreement financing a transaction which is a linked transaction in relation to—

    (i) an agreement falling within paragraph (*a*), or

    (ii) an agreement falling within paragraph (*b*) financing—

        (*aa*) the purchase of any land, or

        (*bb*) the provision of dwellings on any land,

and secured by a land mortgage on the land referred to in paragraph (*a*) or, as the case may be, the land referred to in sub-paragraph (ii)."

There are obvious problems of definition of concepts involved in this provision, as throughout the legislation. At this point, the following definitions should be noticed (s. 189 (1)) :

" ' land ' includes an interest in land . . . " ;

" ' land mortgage ' includes any security charged on land " ;

" ' security ' in relation to an actual or prospective consumer credit agreement . . . means a mortgage, charge, pledge, bond, debenture, indemnity, guarantee, bill, note or other right provided by the debtor . . ., or at his request (express or implied), to secure the carrying out of the obligations of the debtor . . . under the agreement."

It is thought that primary as well as collateral security agreements will be covered notwithstanding the language of the definition. Other expressions used cannot be usefully defined by quotation. The (regulated) agreement of " debtor-creditor-supplier " (defined by s. 12) is explained by J. E. Adams (*loc. cit.*, pp. 97–98) as being—

" . . . either (despite its title) a bipartite agreement between debtor and creditor to finance a transaction between them, where, in effect, the creditor also ' doubles ' as the supplier, or, in general terms, a tripartite agreement where the creditor makes the finance available to the debtor under some existing or intended arrangements or ' understanding ' between the creditor and the supplier."

PAGE
970
et seq.
contd.
The " debtor-creditor " agreement (defined by s. 13) can be explained as one that does not come within the above quotation or " one for refinancing or existing indebtedness of the debtor, not necessarily to the creditor " (J. E. Adams, *loc. cit.*).

Seeking business.—The 1974 Act (ss. 43–54) regulates such preliminaries to mortgages as advertising and canvassing (without being restricted to regulated agreements as above). Thus the form and contents of advertisements will be prescribed if the advertiser carries on " a business in the course of which he provides credit to individuals secured on land " unless they indicate that the credit must exceed £5,000 and that no security of land is required (ss. 43, 44). There are criminal sanctions (s. 167).

Entry into mortgage.—When the mortgage constitutes a regulated agreement, provision is made both for advance disclosure of information (s. 55) and for withdrawal from the prospective agreement cancelling everything including linked transactions (s. 57). In particular, in lieu of being cancellable during a subsequent " cooling off " period (s. 67 (*a*)), a special " opportunity for withdrawal from prospective land mortgage " is afforded by s. 58 :

" (1) Before sending to the debtor or hirer, for his signature, an unexecuted agreement in a case where the prospective regulated agreement is to be secured on land (the ' mortgaged land '), the creditor or owner shall give the debtor or hirer a copy of the unexecuted agreement which contains a notice in the prescribed form indicating the right of the debtor or hirer to withdraw from the prospective agreement, and how and when the right is exercisable, together with a copy of any other document referred to in the unexecuted agreement.

(2) Subsection (1) does not apply to—

(*a*) a restricted-use credit agreement to finance the purchase of the mortgaged land, or

(*b*) an agreement for a bridging loan in connection with the purchase of the mortgaged land or other land."

The significance and the next step in practice are each indicated in s. 61 :

" (2) In addition, where the agreement is one to which s. 58 (1) applies, it is not properly executed unless—

(*a*) the requirements of s. 58 (1) were complied with, and

(*b*) the unexecuted agreement was sent, for his signature, to the debtor or hirer by post not less than seven days after a copy of it was given to him under s. 58 (1), and

(*c*) during the consideration period, the creditor or owner refrained from approaching the debtor or hirer (whether in person, by telephone or letter, or in any other way) except in response to a specific request made by the debtor or hirer after the beginning of the consideration period, and (*d*) no notice of withdrawal by the debtor or hirer was received by the creditor or owner before the sending of the unexecuted agreement.

(3) In subsection (2) (*c*), ' the consideration period ' means the period beginning with the giving of the copy under s. 58 (1) and ending—

(*a*) at the expiry of seven days after the day on which the unexecuted agreement is sent, for his signature, to the debtor or hirer, or

(*b*) on its return by the debtor or hirer after signature by him, whichever first occurs."

The form and contents of regulated mortgages will be prescribed by regulations (s. 60 ; see also s. 105 as to securities), so that precedents must be provided and published for practitioners. Then it is provided (s. 61) that :

" (1) A regulated agreement is not properly executed unless—

(*a*) a document in the prescribed form itself containing all the prescribed terms and conforming to regulations under section 60 (1) is signed in the prescribed manner both by the debtor or hirer and by or on behalf of the creditor or owner, and

(*b*) the document embodies all the terms of the agreement, other than implied terms, and

(*c*) the document is, when presented or sent to the debtor or hirer for signature, in such a state that all its terms are readily legible."

Also provision is made for copies of the documents to be supplied, both unexecuted and executed, within seven days (ss. 62 and 63).

The sanction for failure to comply with any of these provisions is in each case that the mortgage will be improperly executed. The consequence of improper execution is that the mortgage will only be enforceable on an order of the court (s. 65 ; as to the consequences of dismissal of an application for an order, see ss. 105 (7), 106). However, it is emphasised that these provisions as to entry into a regulated mortgage in general do not apply where the mortgage was not made by the creditor in the course of a business carried on by him (ss. 74 (1) (*a*), 189 (1), as to non-commercial agreements).

Remedies, etc.—Assuming due compliance with the provisions so far mentioned, where there is a regulated mortgage the mortgagee's actions during the currency of the mortgage also come under regulation. Thus, before enforcing any term of the mortgage by demanding earlier payment of any sum or recovering possession of any land, the mortgagee must give the mortgagor at least seven days' notice in a prescribed form (s. 76). Further, in the event of breach and termination, provision is made for " default notices " by ss. 87, 88 and 89 as follows :

" *Need for default notice*

87.—(1) Service of a notice on the debtor or hirer in accordance with section 88 (a ' default notice ') is necessary before the

PAGE
970
et seq.
contd.

creditor or owner can become entitled, by reason of any breach by the debtor or hirer of a regulated agreement—

(*a*) to terminate the agreement, or

(*b*) to demand earlier payment of any sum, or

(*c*) to recover possession of any goods or land, or

(*d*) to treat any right conferred on the debtor or hirer by the agreement as terminated, restricted or deferred, or

(*e*) to enforce any security.

(2) Subsection (1) does not prevent the creditor from treating the right to draw upon any credit as restricted or deferred, and taking such steps as may be necessary to make the restriction or deferment effective.

(3) The doing of an act by which a floating charge becomes fixed is not enforcement of a security.

(4) Regulations may provide that subsection (1) is not to apply to agreements described by the regulations."

" *Contents and effect of default notice*

88.—(1) The default notice must be in the prescribed form and specify—

(*a*) the nature of the alleged breach ;

(*b*) if the breach is capable of remedy, what action is required to remedy it and the date before which that action is to be taken ;

(*c*) if the breach is not capable of remedy, the sum (if any) required to be paid as compensation for the breach, and the date before which it is to be paid.

(2) A date specified under subsection (1) must not be less than seven days after the date of service of the default notice, and the creditor or owner shall not take action such as is mentioned in section 87 (1) before the date so specified or (if no requirement is made under subsection (1)) before those seven days have elapsed.

(3) The default notice must not treat as a breach failure to comply with a provision of the agreement which becomes operative only on breach of some other provision, but if the breach of that other provision is not duly remedied or compensation demanded under subsection (1) is not duly paid, or (where no requirement is made under subsection (1)) if the seven days mentioned in subsection (2) have elapsed, the creditor or owner may treat the failure as a breach and section 87 (1) shall not apply to it.

(4) The default notice must contain information in the prescribed terms about the consequences of failure to comply with it.

(5) A default notice making a requirement under subsection (1) may include a provision for the taking of action such as is mentioned in section 87 (1) at any time after the restriction imposed by subsection (2) will cease, together with a statement that the

PAGE
970
et seq.
contd.

provision will be ineffective if the breach is duly remedied or the compensation duly paid."

" Compliance with default notice

89. If before the date specified for that purpose in the default notice the debtor or hirer takes the action specified under section 88 (1) (*b*) or (*c*) the breach shall be treated as not having occurred."

See also s. 98 : duty to give notice of termination (non-default cases).

Also on the mortgagor's side, the mortgagee is under a duty on request to provide the mortgagor with a copy of the executed agreement, and of any document referred to in it, together with a statement of account on payment of a fee of 15p (ss. 77, 78 and 107, 108, only applying to mortgages in the course of a business). In addition, the mortgagor enjoys a statutory right to complete payments ahead of time (s. 94), and to be allowed a rebate on early settlement (s. 95) and to receive in effect redemption figures within a specified period (s. 97).

Two other important sections should be mentioned here. First, s. 113 contains, in effect, an overriding principle that a mortgagee should not enforce his security so as to be benefited, directly or indirectly, to a greater extent than he would be by enforcing the debt without the security. This would appear to apply particularly to curtail the traditional remedy of foreclosure. Second, s. 126 provides generally :

" A land mortgage securing a regulated agreement is enforceable (so far as provided in relation to the agreement) on an order of the court only."

Presumably this will be applied to principal as well as to collateral securities, *sed quaere.* Incidentally, the county court is given exclusive jurisdiction (s. 141).

Finally, notice ss. 173 and 177 :

" Contracting-out forbidden

173.—(1) A term contained in a regulated agreement or linked transaction, or in any other agreement relating to an actual or prospective regulated agreement or linked transaction, is void if, and to the extent that, it is inconsistent with a provision for the protection of the debtor or hirer or his relative or any surety contained in this Act or in any regulation made under this Act.

(2) Where a provision specifies the duty or liability of the debtor or hirer or his relative or any surety in certain circumstances, a term is inconsistent with that provision if it purports to impose, directly or indirectly, an additional duty or liability on him in those circumstances.

(3) Notwithstanding subsection (1), a provision of this Act under which a thing may be done in relation to any person on an

PAGE
970
et seq.
contd.

order of the court or the Director only shall not be taken to prevent its being done at any time with that person's consent given at that time, but the refusal of such consent shall not give rise to any liability."

" *Saving for registered charges*

177.—(1) Nothing in this Act affects the rights of a proprietor of a registered charge (within the meaning of the Land Registration Act 1925), who—

(*a*) became the proprietor under a transfer for valuable consideration without notice of any defect in the title arising (apart from this section) by virtue of this Act, or

(*b*) derives title from such a proprietor.

(2) Nothing in this Act affects the operation of section 104 of the Law of Property Act 1925 (protection of purchaser where mortgagee exercises power of sale).

(3) Subsection (1) does not apply to a proprietor carrying on a business of debt-collecting.

(4) Where, by virtue of subsection (1), a land mortgage is enforced which apart from this section would be treated as never having effect, the original creditor or owner shall be liable to indemnify the debtor or hirer against any loss thereby suffered by him."

This latter provision confines its protection to dealings with registered charges (see L.R.A. 1925, s. 33 (3)) as opposed to other forms of mortgage. The reference to " any defect in the title arising . . . by virtue of this Act " (subs. (1) (*a*)) seems of obscure significance.

990   *First paragraph.*—*Duke* v. *Robson* is reported at [1973] 1 W.L.R. 267.

990   *Second paragraph.*—Reference may be made also to *Waltham Forest London Borough* v. *Webb* (1974), 232 E.G. 462, where the property was sold by the mortgagee-council in possession at a figure insufficient to meet all sums due and the mortgagor alleged but failed to prove undue or improper delay during which prices had fallen.

992–   **Sale by mortgagee to himself or to a person interested.**—In
993   *Williams* v. *Wellingborough Borough Council* (1975), 119 Sol. J. 577 (C.A.), a council tenant had bought a house from the local authority and executed a legal charge in its favour for the balance of the price ; the transfer on sale reserved a right of pre-emption ; only the statutory power of sale was in the legal charge ; the tenant-purchaser-mortgagor fell into arrears with his mortgage instalments and the local authority-mortgagee purported to exercise the power of sale by transferring the house back to itself. It was held that the transfer was null and void because there had been no true sale but a mere re-taking.

PAGE
997   *Last paragraph* and

998   *First paragraph.—Halifax Building Society* v. *Clark*, now reported at [1973] Ch. 307, was distinguished by the Court of Appeal in *First Middlesbrough Trading and Mortgage Co., Ltd.* v. *Cunningham* (1974), 118 Sol. J. 421, which (the day before the 1973 Act was passed) decided that the words " to pay any sums due . . . under the mortgage " should be construed anyway as confined to arrears of instalments.

998   *First paragraph.—*In *Royal Trust Co. of Canada* v. *Markham* (1975), 119 Sol. J. 643 (C.A.), it was held (1) that an order for suspension under s. 36 (2) of the 1970 Act could only be made for a period defined in the order ; there is no power in the court to make an indefinite suspension ; (2) that a mortgagor must provide evidence that he is " likely " to make payment ; and (3) that account can be taken of a mortgagor's proposal to pay the sums due by selling the property.

998   *Second paragraph.—*In *Manchester Unity Trustees* v. *Sadler* [1974] 1 W.L.R. 770, Walton, J., held, after a detailed consideration of the construction of ss. 36, 37 and 38 of the 1970 Act, that the county court retained exclusive jurisdiction over a mortgagee's action for possession of a dwelling-house even though other claims for relief are added (cp. a genuine action for foreclosure with an incidental possession claim).

1006–
1007   **Preliminary remarks as to receipts.—**The view that s. 116 of the L.P.A. 1925 is only applicable to a mortgage by demise and not to a charge by way of legal mortgage, so that a simple receipt would not suffice for the latter, has been held wrong in *Edwards* v. *Marshall-Lee* (1975), *The Times*, 18th June. Brightman, J., is reported as explaining as follows :

> " The only suggested difference between a mortgage by demise and a charge by way of legal mortgage was the existence in the former case of a term of years. Once all the money had been repaid there were no powers or remedies remaining vested in the mortgagee. It followed, therefore, that a simple receipt not complying with s. 115, but nevertheless proving that all moneys had been repaid, discharged the mortgage, whether it was by demise or otherwise, unless, of course, the money was repaid by someone not entitled to the equity of redemption when other consequences might ensue."

In the case, a vacating receipt on a legal charge failed to name the payer but was held to constitute a valid discharge ; consequently a requisition on the point was bad, the vendor had shown title and he was entitled to forfeit the deposit.

1025   *Second paragraph.—*See now the 4th ed. of Megarry and Wade, *Real Property,* at p. 899 *et seq.*

PAGE

1025
contd. See also *Re Wallis & Simmonds (Builders), Ltd.* [1974] 1 W.L.R. 391, noted against pp. 633–635. In the course of his judgment (at p. 398 E/F), Templeman, J., stated his view that :

> " The doctrine is that as a general rule a deposit of title deeds to secure a debt creates a charge on the land ; it does not make any difference whether the debt is owed by the debtor or whether it is owed by somebody else, and the person who deposits the title deeds is in some way acting as a surety. There can be no distinction in logic between the two cases."

Further he held that the presumption that the deposit of title deeds created a charge on the land was rebuttable but that in the case the evidence did not show that a mere naked lien on the documents themselves had been intended.

1039   *Fourth paragraph.*—For the presently relevant rate of corporation tax, see F. (No. 2) A. 1975, s. 27 (1).

1041   *Concurrent interests.*—*Kidson* v. *MacDonald* is now reported fully at [1974] Ch. 206. The decision has been followed by Walton, J., in *Stephenson* v. *Barclays Bank Trust Co., Ltd.* [1975] 1 W.L.R. 882 (noted further against p. 1057) in relation to a trust fund held, following a deed of family arrangement, for the grandchildren of the settlor in equal shares.

1049   *Options.*—See *Randall* v. *Plumb* [1975] 1 W.L.R. 633, noted against p. 1072.

1056   *Third paragraph.*—*Nichols* v. *I.R.C.* has been affirmed *sub nom. Re Nichols* at [1975] 1 W.L.R. 534 (C.A.).

1056   *Settlements.*—Occasion (3) in the text does not mean that capital gains tax can be levied on the whole of the settled property on the death of a life tenant of a fraction (*Pexton* v. *Bell* [1975] 1 W.L.R. 707). Reference should also be made to the statement of Inland Revenue practice at [1973] B.T.R. 414.

1056   *Last paragraph* and

1057   *First paragraph.*—The wording of F.A. 1969, Sched. 19, para. 9, is quite appropriate to cover the position of any beneficiary entitled to end the trust within the rule in *Saunders* v. *Vautier* (1841), 4 Beav. 115, *affd.* Cr. & Ph. 240, i.e., entitled to call for or direct a transfer of the trust property (see *per* Vaisey, J., in *Re Brockbank* [1948] Ch. 206, at pp. 208–209 ; also *Re A.E.G. Unit Trust, Ltd.'s Deed* [1957] Ch. 415). That this is so has been decided by Walton, J., in *Stephenson* v. *Barclays Bank Trust Co., Ltd.* [1975] 1 W.L.R. 882 (noted against p. 1041), who said of the wording (at p. 890)—

> " I think that the definition has been framed, therefore, with the following points in view. (i) The elimination of the trustees' rights of indemnity, because otherwise it would be possible to postpone the payment of capital gains tax indefinitely by keeping alive what might be a very small right indeed. (ii) The elimination of any question as to what were the assets to which a person has become absolutely entitled in the commonest of all cases ; namely, where the trust fund ultimately vests in possession in various persons in various shares. Of course, if, in the event, vesting

1057
contd.

takes place at different times, it appears to me inescapable that the question may still arise. (iii) The definition says ' jointly ' ; it does not say ' together ' . I think this is because it is intended to comprise persons who are, as it were, in the same interest. This is a point which was alluded to by Foster, J., in *Kidson* v. *MacDonald* [1974] Ch. 239. If property is settled upon *A* for life with remainder to *B*, *A* and *B* are 'together' entitled absolutely as against the trustees, but they are not so entitled ' jointly ', ' concurrently ', or ' as tenants in common'. (iv) Finally, of course, the definition is so framed as to require the person who becomes absolutely entitled to be able to give the trustees a good discharge. In a sense, this is the reverse of the penny of absolute entitlement. "

However, the wording would not cover a residuary beneficiary of an unadministered estate (cp. *Cochrane's Executors* v. *I.R.C.* (1974), 49 T.C. 299).

1061

Interest element.—The authorities were considered at length by Megarry, J., in *I.R.C.* v. *Church Commissioners for England* [1975] 1 W.L.R. 251. Certain leasehold reversions had been sold in consideration of rentcharges for a fixed period ; it was held, after the admission of extrinsic evidence, that according to the nature of the transaction no part of the rentcharges was of a capital nature in the hands of the vendor-charity, which was therefore entitled to recover the income tax deducted (see main text, p. 1100).

1063

First paragraph.—At end, add : See also the general observations of Goulding, J., in *Clark* v. *Follett* (1973), 48 T.C. 677, at pp. 702-704 (re short-term capital gains tax) ; in particular a sale can remain at arm's length where market values are rising but a potential vendor refuses to gazump.

1066

First paragraph, line 4.—The reference must now be to the value determined for capital transfer tax (F.A. 1975, Sched. 12, para. 13), which should be based on similar principles and practices. See further the summary against p. 1171 *et seq.*

1068

Penultimate paragraph.—The text is not affected by the amendments made by F.A. 1974, s. 19 and Sched. 1 (see also F. (No. 2) A. 1975, s. 29, continuing a £25,000 limit).

1069

Third and fourth paragraphs.—As to the replacement of estate duty by capital transfer tax, see the summary against p. 1171 *et seq.*

1071

Second paragraph.—At end, add : Following this decision, it appears that the Revenue now allow a trust corporation's withdrawal fee to be set against the notional gain on the termination of a trust (see [1973] B.T.R. 413).

1072

(ii) *Income tax deductions.*—Notice that the restrictions on relief for interest for income tax purposes (see F.A. 1974, s. 12) do not produce corresponding de-restrictions for capital gains tax purposes. There still stands the flat provision that here " no payment of interest shall be allowable " (F.A. 1965, Sched. 6, para. 4 (3), added by I.C.T.A. 1970, Sched. 15, para. 6 (3)).

PAGE

1072   (iii) *Contingent liabilities.*—Paragraph (*b*) of F.A. 1965, Sched. 6,
contd.   para. 15 (1), was considered in *Randall* v. *Plumb* [1975] 1 W.L.R.
633. An option was granted to purchase land which remained
exercisable for a considerable period ; the consideration for the grant
of the option was the payment of £25,000 but this sum was a deposit
only and was repayable in certain circumstances (in effect, after ten
years, without interest, if the purchaser failed to get planning permission). It was accepted that the grant of the option constituted
a disposal of assets for capital gains tax purposes. The question
was whether the contingent liability to repay the £25,000 should be
taken into account in computing the gain. The answer given by
Walton, J., was affirmative since he took the view that the liability
had *not* been assumed as a vendor of land within para. (*b*). Thereafter,
it became a matter of valuation.

1078   *Third paragraph.*—At end, add a reference to F.A. 1965, Sched. 8,
para. 10 (1), as substituted by F. (No. 2) A. 1975, s. 61, in the wake
of *I.R.C.* v. *Montgomery* [1975] 2 W.L.R. 326.

1078   *Penultimate paragraph.*—At end, refer now also to s. 59 of the
F. (No. 2) A. 1975, relating to gilt-edged securities.

1079   E.   EXEMPTIONS AND RELIEFS

Reference only can be made to certain provisions for relief in
respect of agricultural property and for exemption in respect of
historic houses, etc.: see ss. 55 and 56 of the F. (No. 2) A. 1975.

1080   *First paragraph.*—In any case of sale of mortgaged property,
whether by the mortgagee or the mortgagor or his trustee in bankruptcy, the mortgagee will be a stranger to the capital gains tax
liability so that the proceeds of sale are applicable first in discharge
of the mortgage debt (see *Re McMeekin* (1973), 48 T.C. 725).

1081   *First paragraph.*—*Kidson* v. *MacDonald* is now fully reported at
[1974] Ch. 206 and has been followed in *Stephenson* v. *Barclays Bank
Trust Co., Ltd.* [1975] 1 W.L.R. 882 (noted against pp. 1041 and
1057).

1081   **Business premises.**—Land purchased by a manufacturing company
with the intention of building a factory and offices for carrying on
its trade, but sold before being built on, cannot be said to have been
occupied and used for the purpose of the trade within s. 33 ; mere
visits to the site coupled with the intention to build and an application for planning permission do not satisfy the section (*Temperley* v.
Visibell, Ltd. (1974), 49 T.C. 129 ; see the comment at [1974]
B.T.R. 119 by I. D. Barnett).

1082   *Fourth paragraph.*—Substitute for £10,000 and £2,000 the new
figures of £20,000 and £4,000 respectively : F.A. 1974, s. 34.

1082   *Last paragraph.*—*Re Cohen* is reported at [1973] 1 W.L.R. 415
and *Dingle* v. *Turner* at [1972] A.C. 601.

1082
contd.
The capital transfer tax limit is £100,000 on death, or within one year thereof, but otherwise the tax is unlimited : F.A. 1975, Sched. 6, para. 10.

1084   *Last sentence* and

1085   *First sentence.*—The Revenue have allowed a " modest extension " of the twelve months for sale period in recognition of adverse market conditions provided the intention to sell continues (see 233 E.G. 857 (1975)).

1087   *Multiple dwelling-houses.*—The Inland Revenue has conceded that an occupant of tied accommodation, such as a beneficed clergyman, may choose another house owned by him for the purpose of this exemption " provided it is both available to him for residential purposes and he does in fact reside there at regular intervals " (see statement published at [1973] B.T.R. 415, which assumes a discretion in the Revenue whereas s. 29 (7) in terms makes the taxpayer's choice conclusive).

1088   *Penultimate paragraph, final sentence.*—In this situation, the exemption will still be allowed if the matrimonial home is at any time subsequently transferred to the (ex-)wife as part of a financial settlement, provided it has remained the (ex-)wife's only or main residence and the husband has not chosen another dwelling-house for the purposes of this exemption (see Inland Revenue statement published at [1973] B.T.R. 415 ; this applies, of course, vice versa to wife and husband).

1091   *Following second paragraph, insert :*

F.   DEVELOPMENT GAINS AND FIRST LETTING CHARGE

Under the general head of " Capital Gains from Land ", the Finance Act, 1974 (Pt. III, ss. 38–48), primarily introduced the latest legislation designed to divide up and tax down the " planning " profit on a sale of land. Secondarily it deemed much the same for investors who avoid actual gains, despite developing land, by letting instead of selling. These provisions are obviously of considerable concern to conveyancers. Nevertheless it is only appropriate to give a broad outline of them here for two reasons : firstly, it would exceed the function of this supplementary noter-up to attempt detailed and comprehensive accounts of novel taxes even though directed at land ; secondly these taxes are to be temporary— indeed by the time of publication they may very well have become obsolete. It has been announced that these F.A. 1974 taxes are to be discontinued and replaced by a " development land tax " from an appointed day not before the end of 1975 (White Paper on Land, 1974, Cmnd. 5730, also Inland Revenue Statement issued 4th February, 1975). Although considerable information is available about this proposed tax (see White Paper on Development Land Tax, 1975, Cmnd. 6195) at the time of writing, without enacted provisions in their final and complete form, it would be dangerous

PAGE
1091
contd.
to deal with it here. In the meantime the outline indicated will be given and for a fuller exposition reference may be made to Clifford Joseph, Development Gains and First Lettings Tax (Oyez Publishing, 1974).

Development gains tax.—Generally it may be noted first that this tax is uniquely based on retrospective legislation : it dates, in effect, from a statement of intent made by a previous Government (Conservative) which was taken over after an intervening dissolution and election by its successor (Labour). The relevant date is 17th December, 1973 : transactions after that date are subjected to the new tax although it was not finally enacted until 31st July, 1974 (F.A. 1974, s. 38 (1) ; see also s. 45 (1) as to the first lettings tax operating from the same date). There are a few provisions for transitional situations. Thus the value of any authorised development begun before 18th December, 1973, is excluded from development gains tax although only completed afterwards (F.A. 1974, Sched. 3, para. 14). Again there are, in effect, exemptions in respect of conditional contracts entered into before 18th December, 1973, and in respect of disposals under arrangements made before that date (F.A. 1974, Sched. 4, paras. 3 and 4). For these exemptions, the conditional contract must not be at a price depending on value at the time of fulfilment of the condition ; and the arrangements must have been evidenced in writing (*ibid.*). It is assumed, though it is not made explicit, that an option at a fixed price granted before 18th December, 1973, but exercised after that date would be within the conditional contract exemption (cp. F.A. 1971, Sched. 10, para. 10 (2)).

Also generally notice that in substance there is no independent development gains tax as such. The basic principle is that this tax has been grafted on to the capital gains tax rules. Therefore in general there must first be found a chargeable gain for capital gains tax purposes ; then the development gain part can be found and charged at income tax (or corporation tax) rates. There are, of course, some exceptions : for example, there is an exemption available for original beneficiaries under trusts from capital gains tax (see main text, pp. 1080–1081), but there may be liability for development gains tax (F.A. 1974, s. 42). However, it follows from this basic principle that the new development gains tax does not apply to land dealers who will be liable to income tax anyway as traders (see main text, p. 1091 *et seq.*).

The primary charging provision is s. 38 of the F.A. 1974, applying to " any disposal of any interest in land situated in the United Kingdom " after the relevant date (subs. (1)). As a rule the provisions for computing this tax have to be construed as one with the capital gains tax provisions and therefore the various definitions of that tax will be incorporated by reference (F.A. 1974, s. 57 (3) (*c*)). However, for present purposes the following wide definitions, provided by F.A. 1974, s. 44 (1), should be noticed :

" ' interest in land ' means any estate or interest in land, any right in or over land or affecting the use or disposition of land,

PAGE
1091
contd.

and any right to obtain such an estate, interest or right from another which is conditional on that other's ability to grant the estate, interest or right in question, except that it does not include the interest of a creditor (other than a creditor in respect of a rentcharge) whose debt is secured by way of a mortgage, an agreement for a mortgage or a charge of any kind over land, or, in Scotland, the interest of a creditor in a charge or security of any kind over land ;

' land ' includes buildings ".

Further, reference only can be made to the fact that there are lengthy sections designed in effect to catch indirect disposals of interests in land, one through shares in a land-owning company (F.A. 1974, s. 41) and another through equitable interests in settled property (F.A. 1974, s. 42).

Where there is a disposal within s. 38, then so much of any gain accruing as is a " development gain " must be treated not as a capital gain but as income within Case VI of Schedule D (F.A. 1974, s. 38 (2)). Consequently individuals making such a gain will pay the basic and higher rates of income tax but not the additional investment rate (F.A. 1974, Sched. 7, para. 1 ; see also *ibid.*, para. 2, as to spreading back the gain for up to three years). Trustees and personal representatives will pay the basic and the additional rate of tax (F.A. 1974, s. 43). Companies will pay the corporation tax rate (see F.A. 1974, Sched. 7, paras. 3–6, as to advance corporation tax).

A " development gain " means, in effect, the *least* of the following (F.A. 1974, s. 38 (3)) :

(*a*) the net proceeds of the disposal *less* 120 per cent. of the acquisition costs and subsequent expenditure allowable for capital gains tax purposes (see main text at pp. 1063, 1066 *et seq.*) ; *or*

(*b*) the net proceeds of the disposal *less* 110 per cent. of " current use value " (i.e., in effect, the market value of the interest in land on the assumption that any material development would be unlawful : F.A. 1974, Sched. 3, para. 1 ; see *ibid.*, paras. 6–8, for the definition of " material development ") ; this meaning of development gain is not available if any material development has been carried out after 17th December, 1973 (F.A. 1974, Sched. 3, para. 11) ; *or*

(*c*) the chargeable gain *less* the excess of current use value at disposal over current use value at acquisition ; this meaning of development gain is modified where there has been material development after 17th December, 1973, in effect so as to exclude planning permission for and expenditure attributable to the material development.

For the purposes of (*b*) and (*c*), special provision is made for apportioning the current use value on a part disposal (F.A. 1974, Sched. 3, para. 2), essentially in accordance with the formula for capital gains tax purposes (see main text, p. 1051 *et seq.*).

PAGE
1091
contd.
Exemption from development gains tax is provided where the net proceeds of all chargeable disposals does not exceed (*a*) £10,000 for an individual, or his personal representative, or (*b*) £1,000 for a company or for trustees (F.A. 1974, s. 39 (1)). Also there is provision for marginal relief in effect up to double these figures (*ibid.*, s. 39 (2)). Spouses living together are treated as one individual (*ibid.*, s. 39 (3)); disposals *inter se* are disregarded but otherwise only one small disposals exemption or relief is allowed. Equally, a partnership is generally treated as a single individual (*ibid.*, s. 39 (4)).

Provision is also made for development losses (F.A. 1974, s. 40). These are calculated, in effect, as the converse of method (*c*) above of calculating a development gain. Relief must be claimed within two years of the tax year in which the loss accrued and can only be set against income within Case VI of Schedule D.

First letting tax.—As already indicated, part of the taxation statement (of 17th December, 1973) involved a charge to tax on the first letting or occupation of a non-residential building, and was aimed at the investor who develops and retains but lets land. It does not represent a new tax but is merely a device to bring in capital gains tax and as a result development gains tax in appropriate cases.

The primary charging provision is s. 45 (1) of the F.A. 1974, whereby there is a deemed disposal (and immediate reacquisition) at market value by any person with an interest in the land " where after 17th December, 1973, a *chargeable building* is first let or occupied to a *material extent* " after the commencement of development. A " chargeable building " is defined in effect as a separate building, not constructed or adapted for use as a dwelling, which has resulted from or been subject to material development at any time (F.A. 1974, s. 46 (3) and (4), which elaborates the significance of " separate "). A " material extent " means in general more than 25 per cent. of the floor area (F.A. 1974, ss. 45 (2), 46 (7)). Lettings include sub-leases (F.A. 1974, s. 46 (1), not mentioning agreements for leases) and the occupation has to be rateable (F.A. 1974, s. 46 (2)). The deemed disposal produces potentially a notional gain for both capital gains tax and therefore development gains tax purposes (F.A. 1974, s. 45 (1)).

Various exceptions from the first letting charge are made available (F.A. 1974, Sched. 9). For example, a person with an interest in the building will not be liable if he has not granted any leases or if he is not entitled to rents of £5,000 or more per annum (*ibid.*, para. 2 (2)). Nor will there be liability on a person in so far as he is in occupation of the building himself, and no liability at all if his occupation amounts to 90 per cent. of the floor area (*loc. cit.*). Again exemption will follow if within three years after the deemed disposal there is an actual disposal (*ibid.*, para. 8) or a realised intention to occupy (*ibid.*, para. 9). Also the charge does not apply to lettings between members of a group of companies (*ibid.*, para. 11) nor, in effect, where the building is a trader's stock-in-trade (*ibid.*, para. 15).

PAGE

1091
contd.   Finally, a useful right is conferred to pay any capital gains tax
and development gains tax charged in consequence of a deemed
disposal by instalments over eight years but with interest (F.A. 1974,
Sched. 9, para. 14).

1092   *First paragraph.*—The significance of " trade " for tax purposes
was considered in the House of Lords on final appeal in *Ransom* v.
Higgs at [1974] 1 W.L.R. 1594, when certain highly artificial
transactions in land, described as blatant tax avoidance schemes,
were held not to constitute trading (but see now Artificial Transactions in Land, p. 1106 *et seq.*, main text).

1093   *Second paragraph.*—The transactions in *Ransom* v. *Higgs* have
now been held by the House of Lords not to constitute trade :
[1974] 1 W.L.R. 1594.

1093   *Paragraph* (3).—Reference should be made to *Bowie* v. *Reg. Dunn
(Builders), Ltd.* (1974), 49 T.C. 469, where Brightman, J., found
that a particular piece of land had been acquired as a trading asset
and not as an investment, allowing an appeal from the General
Commissioners on the subtle basis that an inference to the contrary
could not be drawn from the primary facts.

1094   *First paragraph.*—After the first sentence, insert a reference to
Pilkington v. *Randall* (1966), 42 T.C. 622, where the taxpayer bought
his sister's undivided share in certain land (which had been devised to
them as tenants in common) with the intention of improving and
selling the land as sole owner.

On appeal in *Taylor* v. *Good* at [1974] 1 All E.R. 1137, the Court
of Appeal qualified and clarified the inferences to be drawn from
the other cases cited.   Almost as an absolute point of law it was in
this case pronounced that where land has been purchased with no
thought of dealing then trading or an adventure in the nature of
trade cannot be found unless some other land has been purchased
with intent to trade.   " If of course you find a trade in the purchase
and sale of land, it may not be difficult to find that properties
originally owned (for example) by inheritance, or bought for investment only, have been brought into the stock-in-trade of that trade "
(*per* Russell, L.J., at [1974] 1 All E.R., p. 1144c).   But without such
an existing trade, it now seems virtually impossible for a taxpayer
to become a trader by changing his mind.   The Court of Appeal
(reversing Megarry, J.) held that the Commissioners' finding of
an adventure in the nature of trade was wrong in law.   Strongly
rejected was the theory " that a man who owns or buys without
present intention to sell land is engaged in trade if he subsequently,
not being himself a developer, merely takes steps to enhance the
value of the property in the eyes of a developer who might wish
to buy for development " (*per* Russell, L.J., at [1974] 1 All E.R.
p. 1143 H/I ; but cp. *ibid.*, p. 1144 F/G, where the possibility of there
being trading was assumed apparently for the sake of argument).
With this case should be compared *Clark* v. *Follett* (1973), 48 T.C. 677,
where the facts were substantially similar—an isolated transaction
of purchase and resale at a profit of a dilapidated farm—but

PAGE
1094
contd.
Goulding, J., had upheld the Commissioners' decision that there was an adventure in the nature of trade. It is thought that this result may have a little difficulty in standing with *Taylor* v. *Good*, *ante*. Neither the case stated nor the facts given in the judgment established the seemingly essential element that the taxpayer had a present intention to sell at the time of his acquisition. On the contrary, his original idea was to reacquire and work his own former farm (see para. (xiv) at 48 T.C., pp. 682–683), and a provisional arrangement was made for resale only if he was unable to finance the reacquisition (see para. (xix) at 48 T.C., pp. 683–684). True, the taxpayer did give instructions for a resale by auction before his purchase had been completed, but this was after the exchange of contracts and on professional advice. The questions of the relevant time of acquisition and the taxpayer's intention at that time were not adverted to in the judgment (see main text, p. 1108, for a similar problem with artificial transactions).

1094 *Penultimate paragraph.*—The decision and reasoning of Megarry, J., in *Ransom* v. *Higgs* has been ultimately reversed by the House of Lords at [1974] 1 W.L.R. 1594.

1095 *First paragraph.*—See *Bowie* v. *Reg. Dunn* (*Builders*), *Ltd.* (1974), 49 T.C. 469, as to the inference from the primary facts being a question of law, not merely of fact.

1095 *Third paragraph.*—*Ransom* v. *Higgs* has reached the House of Lords at [1974] 1 W.L.R. 1594. Reference also should be made to *Clark* v. *Follett* (1973), 48 T.C. 677, where both the purchase and the resale took place in 1964 and Goulding, J., in effect, upheld an assessment under Case I of Sched. D and dismissed an alternative assessment to short-term capital gains tax. The latter assessment had in fact been raised first by the inspector of taxes and it is not made clear by the report of the case why the former was raised at all. This slight mystery is dissipated elsewhere ; apparently the taxpayer himself might have resisted the latter assessment on the ground that the gain was attributable to his trade (see *per* Salmon, L.J., in *R.* v. *Freshwell Commissioners, ex parte Clarke* (1971), 47 T.C. 691, at p. 698 ; same case, different proceedings). This case shows that there may properly be raised alternative assessments, one on profits of a trade and the other on capital gains, notwithstanding the inherent inconsistency of doing so. Will alternative assessments become Revenue practice ? There is still good cause to hope not. Counsel to the Crown in *Clark* v. *Follett, ante,* explained the expected position as follows :

> " As your lordship is well aware, these trading cases do sometimes come very near the border. It is really for that reason that you have got the short-term—now the capital—gains tax provisions, which make the whole thing easier, and you do not have these borderline disputes "

(Mr. Patrick Medd at 48 T.C., p. 706E). Generally, of course, very few taxpayers are likely to resist a capital gains tax assessment (at 30 per cent.) on the ground that they should really be assessed

PAGE
1095
contd.
as traders (i.e., at income tax rates ; in *Clark* v. *Follett* the short-term capital gains tax liability actually would have been at income tax rates under Case VII of Sched. D).

However, where the asset in question was acquired before 1965 it seems that the Revenue may still feel compelled to contest the borderline between capital and income receipts : see *Bowie* v. *Reg. Dunn (Builders), Ltd.* (1974), 49 T.C. 469, where land acquired in 1957 was sold in 1966 and the profit for income tax purposes was computed at £30,869 whereas for capital gains tax purposes it was apparently only £5,807 (presumably because computed only from 6th April, 1965 ; see main text at p. 1076 *et seq.*).

1095
Final paragraph.—The possible application of development gains tax to capital gains must now also be borne in mind (see F.A. 1974, s. 38 ; also Sched. 9, para. 15, purporting to exempt traders ; see also Philip Lawton [1974] B.T.R., at p. 298).

1097
First paragraph.—*Odean Associated Cinemas, Ltd.* v. *Jones* is now reported at [1973] Ch. 288 and *Heather* v. *P.E. Consulting Group, Ltd.* at [1973] Ch. 189.

1100
Rentcharges.—See *I.R.C.* v. *Church Commissioners for England* [1975] 1 W.L.R. 251, noted against p. 1061.

1100–
1101
Stock-in-trade.—Reference for the relief afforded on account of inflation should be made to F.A. 1975, s. 18, and F. (No. 2) A. 1975, s. 54 and Sched. 10.

1104
First paragraph, etc.—*Odeon Associated Cinemas, Ltd.* v. *Jones* is now reported at [1973] Ch. 288 and *Heather* v. *P.E. Consulting Group, Ltd.* at [1973] Ch. 189.

Reference may be made to *Pitt* v. *Castle Hill Warehousing Co., Ltd.* [1974] 1 W.L.R. 1624, where expenditure on a new access road for a trader's premises was held to be capital expenditure ; followed in *E.C.C. Quarries, Ltd.* v. *Watkins* (1975), 119 Sol. J. 562, as to expenditure on planning permission.

1105
Final paragraph.—In the House of Lords in *Ransom* v. *Higgs* at [1974] 1 W.L.R. 1594, some doubt was cast on the total disqualification of dual purpose expenditure, i.e., an appropriate part may be allowable in any case : see *per* Lord Reid at p. 1604 and *per* Lord Cross of Chelsea at p. 1623.

1106
Penultimate paragraph.—The decision in *Ransom* v. *Higgs* has been reversed by the House of Lords at [1974] 1 W.L.R. 1594 and Lord Wilberforce (at p. 1614) stated that the transactions, not being trading, came instead within the present provisions.

1112
Penultimate paragraph.—At end, add : Presumably, however, the mere preparation of plans for development and the making of applications for planning permission cannot mean that " land is developed " within the present provision (cf. *Taylor* v. *Good* [1974] 1 All E.R. 1137 as to trading, noted against p. 1094 ; see also Development Gains Tax, noted against p. 1091).

PAGE

1113   *First paragraph.*—See now also the 8th ed., para. 44–17, of Pinson's Revenue Law.

1115   A. LEASES

It must also not be overlooked that the new development gains tax dealt with against p. 1091 not only has a general application which could catch a proportion of premiums but also imposes a special charge on the first letting of a building after material development.

1117   *Second paragraph.*—*Aplin* v. *White* is reported at [1973] 1 W.L.R. 1311.

1117   *After penultimate paragraph.*—Insert : It should be noticed that where the " usual place of abode " of the lessor is outside the United Kingdom, provision is made for the lessee to deduct tax from payment of rent and then account to the Revenue (I.C.T.A. 1970, s. 89). Lessees who fail to deduct tax in ignorance of their lessors' foreign abode will in practice not be called on to account (see [1974] B.T.R., p. 843).

1119   *Penultimate paragraph.*—After the reference to F.A. 1972, s. 75, add : See now F.A. 1974, s. 19 and Sched. 1 (also F. (No. 2) A. 1975, s. 29, continuing the £25,000 limit).

1120   *Penultimate paragraph.*—*Odeon Associated Cinemas, Ltd*. v. *Jones* is now reported at [1973] Ch. 288 and *Heather* v. *P.E. Consulting Group, Ltd*. at [1973] Ch. 189.

1122   *Penultimate paragraph.*—At end, add : However, a supplementary extra-statutory concession does now allow deduction of such expenditure " where the immediately preceding landlord was the husband or wife (or the trustee for the husband or wife) of the person chargeable or of the person for whom the person chargeable acts as trustee " (see A27 in I.R.1 (insert) (1973) ; the heading to this concession oddly purports to confine it to " property passing from husband to wife (or vice versa) on death ").

1128   *First paragraph.*—*Ball* v. *National and Grindlays Bank, Ltd.* is reported at [1973] Ch. 127.

1132   *First sentence.*—Reference should also be made to *Thompson* v. *Salah* [1972] 1 All E.R. 530.

1145   *First paragraph.*—Delete first sentence, and substitute : In addition, any other (short) lease, treated for VAT purposes as a supply of services, must be broken down in the same way by virtue of the original regulations (see Value Added Tax (General) Regulations, 1972 (S.I. 1972 No. 1147), paras. 18 and 19). Reference should also be made to F.A. 1974, s. 4, which, *inter alia*, covers the position where the lease was granted before the passing of the F.A. 1972.

1147 GROUP 5—FINANCE

Reference may be made to *Customs and Excise Commissioners* v. *Guy Butler (International), Ltd.* [1975] 2 All E.R. 245 concerning the services of a money broker.

1148 GROUP 8—CONSTRUCTION OF BUILDINGS, ETC.

Some relief for " do-it-yourself " builders is afforded by s. 3 of the Finance Act, 1975.

1151 **Conclusion.**—As to the bills of professional gentlemen, see *per* Wien, J., in *Rowe & Maw* v. *Customs and Excise Commissioners* [1975] 2 All E.R. 444, at pp. 447–448 :

" By way of an example, I would say that in many cases a solicitor has to pay out on behalf of his client disbursements which he certainly pays out as an agent. One had in the course of argument the question of stamp duty on a conveyance or an assignment. That is clearly a disbursement made on behalf of the client and would not attract value added tax, because it was a pure disbursement as agent for a principal. But where one gets the case of a solicitor charging as a disbursement, because he is so obliged to do by virtue of the Solicitors' Accounts Rules, something which is not strictly a payment that the client has asked for, either expressly or impliedly, but is part of the whole legal services rendered by the solicitor for which there is a consideration then it seems to me that one must come to the conclusion that there is a taxable supply of legal services which cannot be split up except for accounting purposes."

1151 **A. STAMP DUTIES GENERALLY**

It should be noticed that there is now statutory authority under which stamp duties may be effectively varied or abolished by the House of Commons passing budget resolutions (F.A. 1973, s. 50) ; traditionally, for example, increases or decreases in the rates of conveyance on sale duty have operated as from 1st August, but now an earlier operation may be achieved, as with income tax ; see F.A. 1974, s. 49, Sched. 11, para. 1 (1), whereby the latest increases took effect as from 1st May, 1974. Reference may be made to a note in *Conveyancer N.S.* (1975), vol. 39, at p. 708, as to the effect on certificates of value.

1153 *Sixth paragraph.*—Increase £10,000 to £15,000.

1154 **Duplicates and counterparts.**—As from 1st May, 1974, the stamp is increased to 50p : F.A. 1974, Sched. 11, para. 9.

1158 **Conveyances on sale generally.**—In *Geo. Wimpey & Co., Ltd.* v. *I.R.C.* [1975] 1 W.L.R. 995, at pp. 997–998, Russell, L.J., said :

" Section 54 of the Stamp Act, 1891, so far as relevant, is in these terms : ' For the purposes of this Act the expression " conveyance on sale " includes every instrument . . . whereby any property, or any estate or interest in any property, upon the sale thereof is transferred to or vested in a purchaser, . . . '

PAGE
1158
contd.

The judge, quite rightly on authority, held that s. 54 is applicable in an appropriate case though the instrument creates for the first time the property or the estate or interest in property ; and, as a general proposition, that is not challenged.

In my judgment, the answer to this case is a short one. The instrument in question granted the option to purchase the land pursuant to the recited agreement so to do. The option to purchase is, in my view, within the scope of the word ' property ', which has more than once in the context of the Stamp Act, 1891, been described as a word of wide import. The option was granted for a consideration paid of £15,000. In my view, it is correct to say that the option was sold for that sum by Mr. Morgan and bought for that sum by the taxpayer company. Accordingly, the instrument was one by which property upon the sale thereof was vested in the purchaser of that property, and it was consequently within the expression ' conveyance on sale ' by force of s. 54 and fell to be stamped accordingly."

1159

Fourth paragraph.—Delete all (except the last sentence) and substitute : *Ad valorem* duty is at present charged on a conveyance or transfer on sale of any property at the ordinary rate of £2 per cent. of the consideration; for earlier rates, see Table 2, pp. 110–111, *post*. More precisely this ordinary rate is £1 per £50 or part of £50 of the consideration (see now F.A. 1974, Sched. 11, para. 3) ; for the steps applying if the consideration does not exceed £300, see Table 1, p. 99, *post*.

The ordinary rate is subject to the following special rates :—
Consideration £15,000 or under : duty nil.
Consideration £20,000 or under : rate £½ per cent.
Consideration £25,000 or under : rate £1 per cent.
Consideration £30,000 or under : £1½ per cent.

These special rates are not available where the conveyance is of stock or marketable securities (F.A. 1963, s. 55 (2)).

The special rates are also not available unless the instrument has an appropriate " certificate of value " as follows :

" It is hereby certified that the transaction hereby effected does not form part of a larger transaction or of a series of transactions in respect of which the amount or value or the aggregate amount or value of the consideration exceeds [£15,000] [£20,000] [£25,000] [£30,000] "

(see F.A. 1963, s. 55 (1) (*a*), (*b*), and now F.A. 1974, Sched. 11, para. 4).

1160–
1161

Instruments executed on or after 1st January, 1892, etc.— See now Table 2, *post*, pp. 110–111.

1167

Third, fourth and fifth paragraphs.—Delete and substitute the following :

Leases are now charged with fixed duties in two minor cases and otherwise with *ad valorem* duties (Stamp Act, 1891, s. 1, Sched. 1, as amended by F.A. 1963, s. 56 ; F.A. 1972, s. 125 (3) ; and F.A. 1974, Sched. 11, para. 10).

PAGE
1167
contd.

1. *Fixed duties*

(1) Lease for a definite term less than one year of a furnished dwelling at a total rent for the term exceeding £250 : fixed duty of £1.

Note.—A lease as above but of other premises than a furnished dwelling or at lesser rent is charged *ad valorem* duty as in (2) (*a*) under that heading, *post*, on rent reserved as if a lease for one year at that rent.

(2) Lease of any kind than either (1), *ante*, or those attracting *ad valorem* duty, *post*, fixed duty of £2.

2. *Ad valorem duties*

When a lease is for any definite period other than as above or is an indefinite (i.e., periodic) tenancy, then *ad valorem* duties are charged as follows :

(1) *On any premium :* conveyance on sale duty at the ordinary rate (see note against p. 1159) ; the special rates are applicable only if the rent does not exceed £150 per annum (F.A. 1963, s. 55 (2) ; F.A. 1972, s. 125 (3)) and then the certificate of value has reference to the amount or value of the consideration other than rent. For the previous position, see Table 6, p. 115, *post*.

(2) *On any rent :* the following rates are now calculated on the average rent per annum. For the previous rates, see Table 6, p. 115, *post*.

(*a*) Term not exceeding seven years or periodic : rent not exceeding £250 per annum : duty nil ; otherwise : rate £1 per cent.

(*b*) Term exceeding seven years but not exceeding thirty-five years : rate £2 per cent.

(*c*) Term exceeding thirty-five years but not exceeding one hundred years : rate £12 per cent.

(*d*) Term exceeding one hundred years : rate £24 per cent.

(F.A. 1963, s. 56 (1), Sched. 11, Pt. II ; F.A. 1972, s. 125 (3) ; F.A. 1974, Sched. 11, para. 10).

Details of the steps by which these rates rise are shown in Table 4, p. 112, *post*.

**1171–
1180**

PART 6. ESTATE DUTY/CAPITAL TRANSFER TAX

For deaths on and after 13th March, 1975, estate duty has been abolished and is replaced by capital transfer tax (F.A. 1975, s. 49 (1) ; also estate duty on deaths after 12th November, 1974, was at capital transfer tax rates and otherwise modified retrospectively : *loc. cit.* and Sched. 11 ; also s. 49 (2) and Sched. 8, Pt. II). All that can be attempted in this Supplement is a broad account of the new tax as a background but including a consideration of certain points of concern to conveyancers (i.e., comparable to the rules of estate duty to which attention was drawn in the main text).

General.—As with estate duty, so with capital transfer tax, there are essentially three questions to be answered : first, " Is there a charge ? ", which depends on the statutory provisions as to the levy of tax and as to exemptions ; second, " If so, how much ? ", which depends on the rules as to rates of tax and as to valuation ; and third, " Who pays ? ", which depends on the principles both of accountability and of incidence.

Levy.—Primarily the new tax catches what used to be known for estate duty purposes as a gift *inter vivos* and does so without any dependence on the donor's death. However, the terms of the tax show no similarity to those of the replaced estate duty legislation. The levy is briefly imposed by s. 19 (1) of the F.A. 1975, as follows :

" A tax, to be known as capital transfer tax, shall be charged on the value transferred by a chargeable transfer."

Then this charge is less briefly explained in the next section :

" A chargeable transfer is any transfer of value made by an individual after 26th March, 1974, other than an exempt transfer " (s. 20 (5)).

This calls for further explanations :

" . . . a transfer of value is any disposition made by a person . . . as a result of which the value of his estate immediately after the disposition is less than it would be but for the disposition ; and the amount by which it is less is the value transferred " (s. 20 (2)).

Thus the charge is not on the benefit received but on the overall loss suffered by the transferor, which is very much a matter of valuation (see below) and is subject also to exemptions and exclusions (see below).

It is also obvious that the charge depends on there being a " disposition " and no general definition of this vital word is provided. However, two particular aspects with a tax-avoidance flavour are elaborated. Firstly the interpretation section states that " ' disposition ' includes a disposition effected by associated operations " (s. 51 (1) of the F.A. 1975) and by s. 44 of the Act—

" (1) In this Part of this Act ' associated operations ' means, subject to subsection (2) below, any two or more operations of any kind, being—

(a) operations which affect the same property, or one of which affects some property and the other or others of which affect property which represents, whether directly or indirectly, that property, or income arising from that property, or any property representing accumulations of any such income ; or

(b) any two operations of which one is effected with reference to the other, or with a view to enabling the other to be

PAGE
1171–
1180
contd.

effected or facilitating its being effected, and any further operation having a like relation to any of those two, and so on ;

whether those operations are effected by the same person or different persons, and whether or not they are simultaneous ; and ' operation ' includes an omission.

(2) The granting of a lease for full consideration in money or money's worth shall not be taken to be associated with any operation effected more than three years after the grant, and no operation effected on or after 27th March 1974 shall be taken to be associated with an operation effected before that date.

(3) Where a transfer of value is made by associated operations carried out at different times it shall be treated as made at the time of the last of them ; but where any one or more of the earlier operations also constitute a transfer of value made by the same transferor, the value transferred by the earlier operations shall be treated as reducing the value transferred by all the operations taken together, except to the extent that the transfer constituted by the earlier operations but not that made by all the operations taken together is exempt under paragraph 1 of Schedule 6 to this Act."

(Schedule 6, para. 1, exempts transfers between spouses : as to operations now expressly including omissions, see *Nichols* v. *I.R.C.* [1973] 3 All E.R. 632.) And secondly the ordinary meaning of " disposition " is extended (by s. 20 (7))—

" where the value of a person's estate is diminished and that of another person's estate is increased by the first-mentioned person's omission to exercise a right he shall be treated as having made a disposition at the time, or the latest time, when he could have exercised the right, unless it is shown that the omission was not deliberate."

Otherwise, the word " disposition " will have to be construed and applied to the transaction, so some similar questions could arise to those raised over the words " disposal of " for capital gains tax purposes (see main text, p. 1045 *et seq.*). Notice in particular that a disclaimer would appear to be within s. 20 (7) quoted above as involving a deliberate omission to exercise rights (see also s. 47 (2), (4)), but that other circumstances are less clear. For example, would that subsection cover an option to purchase land which is not exercised because of a lack of planning permission or of finance ? Again, equal difficulty may be experienced with uncompleted contracts and forfeited deposits (but see s. 20 (4), below). A more common question for conveyancers in a period of fluctuating land values could be whether the disposition is constituted by the contract or by the conveyance. The answer seems to be that the contract will be the disposition. This is inferred from s. 40 of the Act, applying :

" (1) Where a disposition made for a consideration in money or money's worth is a transfer of value and any payments made

PAGE
1171–
1180
contd.
or assets transferred by the transferor in pursuance of the disposition are made or transferred more than one year after the disposition is made . . ."

By this section, following a contract for sale of land at undervalue or overvalue (i.e., a gift of value one way or the other), if completion is delayed over a year, then appropriate separate dispositions will be deemed to be made. But the section does not apply where completion is within the year nor where the contract was at market value ; so a contract to sell land worth say £20,000 for £20,000 which is completed when the land's value has inflated to say £40,000 (or depreciated to £10,000) might prove a useful arrangement.

In addition, of course, a disposition for full consideration will not be a transfer of value (see s. 20 (2), above). Further, however, where there is less than full consideration it is also provided (s. 20 (4))—

"A disposition is not a transfer of value if it is shown that it was not intended, and was not made in a transaction intended, to confer any gratuitous benefit on any person and either—

(a) that it was made in a transaction at arm's length between persons not connected with each other, or

(b) that it was such as might be expected to be made in a transaction at arm's length between persons not connected with each other."

(not applying fully to dispositions of reversionary interests or of unquoted shares). Thus if the necessary subjective intention and objective expectation can be shown, a " bad bargain " exemption in effect may be established.

Apart from the primary charge on actual gifts inter vivos or transfers of value, such gifts or transfers are deemed to occur and be chargeable in certain circumstances. A relevant but comparatively minor example is provided by s. 41 (marginal note : " Free loans, etc.") :

"(1) Where a person, otherwise than in a transaction at arm's length between persons not connected with each other, allows another the use of money or other property without consideration in money or money's worth or for a consideration less than could reasonably be expected in such a transaction, he shall be treated as making a transfer of value in every chargeable period in which he allows that use ; and—

(a) the value transferred thereby shall be the difference between the amount of the consideration (if any) for that period and that of the consideration that might be so expected ; and

(b) the transfer shall be treated as being made at the end of the chargeable period or, if earlier, at the time when that use comes to an end ; and

(c) the transfer shall be treated as made out of the transferor's income.

(2) In this section ' chargeable period ', in relation to any use, means the period beginning when the use is begun and ending with 5th April next following, and every subsequent period of twelve months ending with 5th April, but no period beginning before 6th April 1976 shall be a chargeable period."

This provision seems potentially very wide, able to cover, for example, any licence to occupy land otherwise than for full consideration (e.g., rent-free living accommodation) as well as such benefits as interest-free loans of money. Note that its operation is postponed until 6th April, 1976, *semble* with a view to amendment. Another example is the section designed to deal with gifts via close companies (s. 39). But the main example of deeming occurs on death, i.e., directly replacing the principal charge to estate duty on property of which the deceased was competent to dispose (s. 2 (1) (a) of the F.A. 1894).

Accordingly, the secondary levy is under the following provision (s. 22 (1) of the F.A. 1975) :

" On the death of any person after the passing of this Act tax shall be charged as if, immediately before his death, he had made a transfer of value and the value transferred by it had been equal to the value of his estate immediately before his death, but subject to the following provisions of this section."

Subsections (2) and (3) provide for a reverter to settlor or to settlor's spouse exemption (i.e., as for estate duty under F.A. 1896, s. 15, but with modifications). The remaining sections contain various transitional provisions, except for subs. (9), which avoids a double charge in a *commorientes* situation by providing :

" For the purposes of this section, where it cannot be known which of two or more persons who have died survived the other or others they shall be assumed to have died at the same instant."

(See also s. 30 of the Act, providing some quick death relief for certain situations.)

The meaning of " a person's estate ", which must be understood for gifts *inter vivos* as well as for transfers on death (see s. 20 (2) above), is explained as follows (s. 23 (1)) :

" For the purposes of this Part of this Act, a person's estate is the aggregate of all the property to which he is beneficially entitled, except that the estate of a person immediately before his death does not include excluded property."

This should be read with para. 3 (1) of Sched. 5 (relating to settled property), which provides :

" A person beneficially entitled to an interest in possession in settled property shall be treated as beneficially entitled to the property in which the interest subsists."

Thus the death of a life tenant or other person with a limited interest in possession produces a charge on the settled property itself, not just on the value of that interest (i.e., the equivalent of the estate

PAGE
1171–
1180
contd.

duty charges under s. 2 (1) (*b*) of the F.A. 1894, as amended ; see also para. 4 (1) of Sched. 5 as to termination of such interest *inter vivos*). There is also a provision bringing into a person's estate property over which he has a general power of appointment (s. 23 (2), not applying *semble* to special, joint, consent or other hybrid powers even though the appointment could be in his own favour). Excluded, but not to confer any exemption, is a reversionary interest acquired by a person with a prior interest (s. 23 (3) ; cp. s. 38 of the F.A. 1969, main text, p. 1178).

Apart from the charges on actual gifts *inter vivos* and on deemed transfers of value, including on death, a third variety of charge arises where a capital distribution is made, actually or notionally, out of settled property. The outline principles in applying capital transfer tax to settled property are :

(1) on the creation of the settlement the ordinary gift *inter vivos* or transfer on death rules apply ;

(2) so long as there is someone with a beneficial interest in possession, the charging rules apply as if he were the owner of the settled property (see Sched. 5, para. 3 (1), referred to above) ;

(3) if there is *no* interest in possession (e.g., especially where there is a discretionary trust) a charge to tax is made—

   (A) on every payment out of the settled property (Sched. 5, para. 6), and

   (B) on the value of the settled property itself, in general, at ten-year intervals (Sched. 5, para. 12) ;

these are respectively actual and notional capital distributions ; there are miscellaneous other circumstances in which a capital distribution is deemed made ; there are also miscellaneous exemptions, e.g., accumulation and maintenance settlements, trusts for benefit of employees, etc., protective trusts, charitable trusts (see Sched. 5 *et seq.*).

No further details will be gone into here ; note only that Sched. 5, which deals with the application of the tax to settled property, has been authoritatively said to contain " the most complicated provisions of capital transfer tax " (Wheatcroft and Hewson, Capital Transfer Tax, 1975, para. 6–01). However, the attention of conveyancers is drawn particularly to the point that the definitions of settled property and settlement for capital transfer tax purposes do *not* include trusts under which simple concurrent interests are enjoyed (see Sched. 5, para. 1 (2), referring to successive and contingent interests, to accumulation and discretionary trusts and to annuities). Also notice that leases for lives are to be treated as settlements unless granted for full consideration in money or money's worth (*ibid.*, para. 1 (3)).

Finally, a charge to capital transfer tax will arise on breach of certain undertakings given to the Treasury as a condition of exemption relating to works of art, etc., and buildings of special interest, etc. (see ss. 32 and 34 ; cp. also Sched. 9, para. 2, as to disposal of trees or underwood).

PAGE
1171–
1180
contd.

Exemptions.—Where there would *prima facie* be a charge to capital transfer tax because of the application of the provisions making the levy, the next step is to consider whether the transfer in question may not be chargeable because it is exempt (see s. 20 (5) of the F.A. 1975 : ". . . other than an exempt transfer "). Schedule 6 to the 1975 Act sets out the detailed provisions as to exempt transfers. These include most but not all of the known estate duty exemptions in similar terms and are not generally of particular concern in ordinary conveyancing. Accordingly only the Sched. 6 headings will be given here by way of indication and for reference purposes :

(i) Transfer between spouses (para. 1).

(ii) Values not exceeding £1,000 (paras. 2 and 3—" in any one year ").

(iii) Small gifts to same person (para. 4—£100 " in any one year ").

(iv) Normal expenditure out of income (para. 5).

(v) Gifts in consideration of marriage (paras. 6 and 7 —maximum £5,000 by parent).

(vi) Transfers in course of trade, etc. (para. 9—this is new, depends on the value being deductible for income tax purposes, and consequently seems unnecessary since there should then be no " gratuitous benefit " intended within s. 20 (4) of the Act).

(vii) Gifts to charities (para. 10—limited to £100,000 on death or within one year before but otherwise unlimited ; see the useful peculiarity referred to in the main text, p. 1082, last paragraph).

(viii) Gifts to political parties (para. 11).

(ix) Gifts for national purposes, etc. (para. 12).

(x) Gifts for public benefit (para. 13).

(xi) Gifts made before 10th December, 1974, and not relevant to estate duty (para. 14).

It is assumed that these exemptions are cumulative, although there is nothing in the statute to support the assumption.

Apart from this list of exempt transfers, Sched. 7 to the Act also sets out certain miscellaneous exemptions and reliefs, under the following headings :

(i) Death on active service, etc. (para. 1).

(ii) Cash option under approved annuity schemes (para. 2).

(iii) Government securities free of tax whilst in foreign ownership (para. 3).

(iv) Overseas pensions (para. 4).

(v) Savings by persons domiciled in Channel Islands or Isle of Man (para. 5).

(vi) Visiting forces and staff of allied headquarters (para. 6).

(vii) Double taxation relief (para. 7).

PAGE
1171–
1180
contd.

Most of these are not merely a matter of an exempt transfer but constitute "excluded property", either expressly ((iii), (v) and (vi)) or *semble* impliedly.   No account is taken of excluded property in determining whether there is a chargeable transfer of value (see ss. 20 (3), 23 (1) of the 1975 Act).   In addition to the Sched. 7 instances of excluded property and to foreign settled property (Sched. 5, para. 2, unless the settlor had a U.K. domicile), it is also provided (by s. 24) that :

" (2) Property situated outside the United Kingdom is excluded property if the person beneficially entitled to it is an individual domiciled outside the United Kingdom.

(3) A reversionary interest is excluded property unless—

(*a*) it has at any time been acquired (whether by the person entitled to it or by a person previously entitled to it) for a consideration in money or money's worth ; or

(*b*) it is the interest expectant on the determination of a lease treated as a settlement by virtue of paragraph 1 (3) of Schedule 5 to this Act."

(An extended meaning is given to domicile by s. 45 of the 1975 Act.) Subsection (3) follows logically from the principle already mentioned that a person with a beneficial interest in possession is treated as the owner of the settled property (Sched. 5, para. 3 (1)).

Also an exemption is provided under the heading " *Disposition for maintenance of family* " in respect of spouses, former spouses, their children (under eighteen or still being educated ; step, adopted or illegitimate), and dependent relatives (s. 46).   In addition, of more direct concern to conveyancers, is a provision incidentally facilitating in effect retrospective family estate planning (s. 47) :

" (1) So far as a deed of family arrangement or similar instrument which is made not more than two years after the death of any person varies the dispositions (whether effected by will or under the law relating to intestacy) of the property of which he was competent to dispose—

(*a*) the variation shall not be a transfer of value ; and

(*b*) this Part of this Act shall apply as if the variation had been effected by the deceased.

(2) Where a legacy or any interest in a deceased person's estate is disclaimed within two years of his death and the disclaimer is not made for a consideration in money or money's worth, the disclaimer is not a transfer of value.

(3) An election by a surviving spouse under section 47A of the Administration of Estates Act 1925 (redemption of life interest in residuary estate) is not a transfer of value ; and where such an election is made this Part of this Act shall have effect as if the surviving spouse, instead of being entitled to the life interest, had been entitled to a sum equal to the capital value mentioned in that section.

PAGE
1171–
1180
contd.

(4) Where a person becomes entitled to an interest in settled property but disclaims the interest, then, if the disclaimer is not made for a consideration in money or money's worth, this Part of this Act shall apply as if he had not become entitled to the interest.

(5) In relation to a death occurring before the passing of this Act but not before 10th December, 1972, subsection (1) above shall have effect as if the reference to a deed of family arrangement or similar instrument made not more than two years after the death were a reference to such a deed or instrument made not more than two years after the passing of this Act."

The odd flaw is that no definition has been provided of the vital expression " a deed of family arrangement ", which leaves an area for argument.

Further, certain other exemptions are available which have been referred to in passing above : the "bad bargain" (s. 20 (4)) ; reverter to settlor or his spouse (s. 22 (2), (3)) ; miscellaneous in respect of capital distributions under settlements (Sched. 5, para. 15 *et seq.*) ; and conditionally in respect of works of art, etc., and buildings of special interest, etc. (ss. 32, 34).

Lastly it must be noticed that the estate duty " exemption for certain property passing by reason of purchase ", dealt with on p. 1179 of the main text, has *not* been repeated for capital transfer tax purposes.

Rate of tax.—This is governed generally by s. 37 of the Act as follows :

" (1) The tax charged on the value transferred by a chargeable transfer made by any transferor shall be charged at the following rate or rates, that is to say—

(*a*) if the transfer is the first chargeable transfer made by that transferor, at the rate or rates applicable to that value under the appropriate Table set out in subsection (3) below ;

(*b*) if the transfer is not the first chargeable transfer made by that transferor, at the rate or rates applicable under that Table to such part of the aggregate of that value and of the values previously transferred by chargeable transfers made by that transferor, as is the highest part of that aggregate and is equal to that value.

(2) Except as otherwise provided, the First Table set out in subsection (3) below is the appropriate Table for a transfer made on or at any time within three years of the death of the transferor, and the Second Table set out in that subsection is the appropriate Table for any other transfer.

(3) In each of the Tables set out below any rate shown in the third column is that applicable to such portion of the value concerned as exceeds the lower limit shown in the first column but does not exceed the upper limit (if any) shown in the second column.

PAGE
1171–
1180
contd.

FIRST TABLE

Portion of value		Rate of tax
Lower limit £	Upper limit £	Per cent.
0	15,000	Nil
15,000	20,000	10
20,000	25,000	15
25,000	30,000	20
30,000	40,000	25
40,000	50,000	30
50,000	60,000	35
60,000	80,000	40
80,000	100,000	45
100,000	120,000	50
120,000	150,000	55
150,000	500,000	60
500,000	1,000,000	65
1,000,000	2,000,000	70
2,000,000	—	75

SECOND TABLE

Portion of value		Rate of tax
Lower limit £	Upper limit £	Per cent.
0	15,000	Nil
15,000	20,000	5
20,000	25,000	$7\frac{1}{2}$
25,000	30,000	10
30,000	40,000	$12\frac{1}{2}$
40,000	50,000	15
50,000	60,000	$17\frac{1}{2}$
60,000	80,000	20
80,000	100,000	$22\frac{1}{2}$
100,000	120,000	$27\frac{1}{2}$
120,000	150,000	35
150,000	200,000	$42\frac{1}{2}$
200,000	250,000	50
250,000	300,000	55
300,000	500,000	60
500,000	1,000,000	65
1,000,000	2,000,000	70
2,000,000	—	75 ”

PAGE
1171–
1180
contd.

Two aspects of this provision should be especially appreciated. Firstly, the rates have reference to the cumulative total of transfers of value. Secondly, although a lower rate is attracted by gifts *inter vivos* until three years before death, this is offset by a grossing-up effect if the donor bears the capital transfer tax himself, i.e., it too becomes part of the whole value transferred in the statutory sense of lessening the value of the transferor's estate (see s. 20 (2) and Sched. 10, para. 1 (2)).

A lower rate, in effect, is attracted in two circumstances : firstly, where the deemed periodic capital distribution of settled property occurs (i.e., there being no interest in possession ; e.g., a discretionary trust), it is charged at 30 per cent. of the rate otherwise chargeable (Sched. 5, para. 12 (1)) ; secondly, by virtue of transitional relief provided for settlements made before 27th March, 1974, in general capital distributions, actual or notional, made before 1st April, 1980, out of settled property are to be charged at the following percentages of the rates which would otherwise be chargeable (Sched. 5, para. 14 (2)) :

" (*a*) 10 per cent. if the capital distribution is made before 1st April, 1976 ;

(*b*) 12½ per cent. if it is made after 31st March, 1976, but before 1st April, 1977 ;

(*c*) 15 per cent. if it is made after 31st March, 1977, but before 1st April, 1978 ;

(*d*) 17½ per cent. if it is made after 31st March, 1978, but before 1st April, 1979 ; and

(*e*) 20 per cent. if it is made after 31st March, 1979."

Valuation.—It must first be appreciated that for gifts *inter vivos* the question is not simply one of valuing the property transferred : the relevant question is the difference in the value of the donor's estate before and after the gift (s. 20 (2) of the 1975 Act). For a transfer on death, what has to be ascertained is the aggregate " value of his estate immediately before his death " (s. 22 (1)). The reference to a person's estate brings in the familiar estate duty principle of aggregation of the values of all his own property (see s. 23 (1)). For capital transfer tax purposes, it is provided generally (s. 38 (1)) that :

" (1) Except as otherwise provided by this Part of this Act, the value at any time of any property shall for the purposes of capital transfer tax be the price which the property might reasonably be expected to fetch if sold in the open market at that time ; but that price shall not be assumed to be reduced on the ground that the whole property is to be placed on the market at one and the same time."

Thus generally the estate duty valuation rules would appear to remain applicable, but differences may emerge. For example, here the time as at which a deceased's estate must be valued is " immediately before his death " (s. 23 (1)), whereas for estate duty purposes the relevant time has been held by the House of Lords

PAGE
1171–
1180
contd.

to be as at the moment after death (*I.R.C.* v. *Graham's Trustees* (1970), 115 Sol. J. 681). Also a considerable number of detailed rules as to valuation in particular circumstances and of particular assets are contained in Sched. 10 to the 1975 Act.

Accountability —Liability for paying capital transfer tax to the Inland Revenue is governed primarily by the provisions of s. 25 of the 1975 Act ; reference should be made to Sched. 4 for detailed provisions as to the administration and collection of the tax.

First, where there is a chargeable gift *inter vivos*, the persons liable (by s. 25 (2)) are :

" (*a*) the transferor and the transferee ; and

(*b*) so far as the tax is attributable to the value of any property, any person in whom the property is vested (whether beneficially or otherwise) at any time after the transfer or who at any such time is beneficially entitled to an interest in possession in the property ; and

(*c*) where by the chargeable transfer any property becomes comprised in a settlement, any person for whose benefit any of the property or income from it is applied."

Second, where the charge is in relation to settled property, the persons liable (by s. 25 (3)) are :

" (*a*) the trustees of the settlement ; and

(*b*) any person entitled (whether beneficially or not) to an interest in possession in the settled property ; and

(*c*) any person for whose benefit any of the settled property or income from it is applied at or after the time of the transfer ; and

(*d*) where the chargeable transfer is made during the life of the settlor and the trustees are not for the time being resident in the United Kingdom, the settlor."

Where several persons are liable as above, each of them is liable to pay the whole tax (s. 25 (1) ; it may be recoverable : see s. 28). Here, however, the primary liability is on the transferor/donor and the settlor, the liability of the others being limited, in effect, to the unpaid balance (s. 27 (6)), except where the chargeable transfer was within three years of his death when the donor's or settlor's liability is limited (s. 25 (4)).

Third, if the transfer was on death, the persons liable (by s. 25 (5)) are :

" (*a*) so far as the tax is attributable to the value of property which either—

(i) was not immediately before the death comprised in a settlement ; or

(ii) was so comprised and consists of land in the United Kingdom which devolves upon or vests in the deceased's personal representatives,

the deceased's personal representatives ;

PAGE
1171–
1180
contd.

(b) so far as the tax is attributable to the value of property which, immediately before the death, was comprised in a settlement, the trustees of the settlement ;

(c) so far as the tax is attributable to the value of any property, any person in whom the property is vested (whether beneficially or otherwise) at any time after the death or who at any such time is beneficially entitled to an interest in possession in the property ;

(d) so far as the tax is attributable to the value of any property which, immediately before the death, was comprised in a settlement, any person for whose benefit any of the property or income from it is applied after the death ;

and for the purposes of this subsection a person entitled to part only of the income of any property shall, notwithstanding anything in paragraph 3 of Schedule 5 to this Act, be deemed to be entitled to an interest in the whole of the property."

In addition, for liability to tax, both an executor *de son tort* and the manager of property for a person not of full legal capacity are to be treated as persons in whom the property is vested (s. 25 (6)).

Certain exceptions from liability of particular concern to purchasers are afforded by s. 26 and are dealt with separately below. Also the liability generally of trustees and personal representatives and of persons in whom the property is vested or for whom settled property is applied is limited to the value of the property which they received or ought to have received (s. 27).

Purchaser's concern with capital transfer tax.—In substance, the position is very much the same as it was for death duties (see main text, pp. 1171–1173) ; i.e., a purchaser or mortgagee should only be concerned if a charge for tax has been registered. *Prima facie*, of course, a purchaser, etc., would be potentially liable to pay the tax as "any person in whom the property is vested (whether beneficially or otherwise) at any time" after the gift or death in question (i.e., within s. 25 (2) (b) and (5) (c)). However, it is provided (by s. 26 (1)) that:

"A purchaser of property, and a person deriving title from or under such a purchaser, shall not by virtue of subsection (2) (b) or (5) (c) of section 25 of this Act be liable for tax attributable to the value of the property, unless the property is subject to an Inland Revenue charge."

And for present purposes "purchaser" is defined (s. 51 (1)) as meaning :

"a purchaser in good faith for consideration in money or money's worth other than a nominal consideration and includes a lessee, mortgagee or other person who for such consideration acquires an interest in the property in question".

The Inland Revenue charge for unpaid tax following a gift *inter vivos* or a death is (by Sched. 4, para. 20 (1)) on :

"(a) any property to the value of which the value transferred is wholly or partly attributable ; and

PAGE
1171–
1180
contd.

      (b) where the chargeable transfer is made by the making of a
          settlement or is made under Schedule 5 to this Act, any
          property comprised in the settlement."

(And this expressly extends to a charge on any property directly
or indirectly representing that property : para. 20 (2).)   However,
sub-para. (1) (a) appears difficult to apply : the intent may have been
that the charge should essentially be on the property transferred but
unfortunately for this the value transferred *inter vivos* is made
attributable to all the donor's property before and after the transfer
(ss. 20 (2), 23 (1)) ; i.e., the charge could be on all his estate.   The
charge cannot normally be on the whole of a deceased's estate
because it is provided (by Sched. 4, para. 20 (3)) that :

> " Where the chargeable transfer is made on death, personal
> or movable property situated in the United Kingdom which was
> beneficially owned by the deceased immediately before his death
> and vests in his personal representatives is not subject to the
> Inland Revenue charge ; and for this purpose ' personal property '
> includes leaseholds and undivided shares in land held on trust
> for sale, whether statutory or not, and the question whether any
> property was beneficially owned by the deceased shall be deter-
> mined without regard to paragraph 3 (1) of Schedule 5 to this
> Act."

Thus the charge following a death will obviously be on realty and
foreign property, but also on settled property and on property over
which the deceased had an *un*-exercised general power of appointment (cp. *O'Grady* v. *Wilmot* [1916] 2 A.C. 231).   On the death of a
beneficial joint tenant of land, presumably he is deemed to have
disposed of his severable share immediately before his death
(ss. 22 (1), 23 (1)) ; *semble* no deemed severance occurs and the
valuation disregards the accrual by survivorship (Sched. 10,
para. 9 (1) (a) and (2)).   Query : should the valuation immediately
before death also disregard, e.g., a terminal illness, leading to such
accrual?   The severable share will be personal property, i.e.,
necessarily an interest in the proceeds of sale, but since it does
not pass to the deceased joint tenant's general representatives
it will be subject to a charge (see further main text, pp. 1174–1176).

The protection for a purchaser is provided (by Sched. 4, para. 21)
as follows :

> " (1) Where property subject to an Inland Revenue charge, or
> an interest in such property, is disposed of to a purchaser, then if
> at the time of the disposition—
>
> (a) in the case of land in England and Wales, the charge was
>   not registered as a land charge or, in the case of registered
>   land, was not protected by notice on the register ; or
>
> [para. (b) refers to land in Northern Ireland]
>
> (c) in the case of personal property situated in the United
>   Kingdom other than such property as is mentioned in

PAGE
1171–
1180
contd.

paragraph (a) above, and of any property situated outside the United Kingdom, the purchaser had no notice of the facts giving rise to the charge ; or

(d) in the case of any property, a certificate of discharge had been given by the Board under this Schedule and the purchaser had no notice of any fact invalidating the certificate,

the property or interest shall then cease to be subject to the charge but the property for the time being representing it shall be subject to it.

(2) Where property subject to an Inland Revenue charge, or an interest in such property, is disposed of to a purchaser in circumstances where it does not then cease to be subject to the charge, it shall cease to be subject to it on the expiration of the period of six years beginning with the later of the following dates, namely—

(a) the date on which the tax became due ; and

(b) the date on which a full and proper account of the property was first delivered to the Board in connection with the chargeable transfer concerned.

(3) In this paragraph ' the time of the disposition ' means—

(a) in relation to registered land, the time of registration of the disposition ; and

(b) in relation to other property, the time of completion."

Notice that consequential amendments have been made to the L.C.A. 1972 (by Sched. 12, para. 18, to the 1975 Act). Accordingly, if an Inland Revenue charge is protected by registration and revealed by a land charges search, the purchaser should require production of a certificate of discharge as indicated on p. 1171 of the main text but now under Sched. 4, para. 25.

In the case of registered land, the position indicated for death duties on p. 1172 of the main text is *not* true for capital transfer tax : the charge is *not* now overreached in favour of a purchaser. A new s. 73 of the Land Registration Act, 1925, has been substituted in the following terms (by Sched. 12, para. 5)—

" A disposition shall take effect subject to any subsisting Inland Revenue charge under Part III of the Finance Act 1975 unless—

(a) the disposition is in favour of a purchaser within the meaning of that Part ; and

(b) the charge is not, at the time of registration of the disposition, protected by notice on the register."

(See also the new rr. 191, 192 and 193 and Forms 60 and 61 of the Land Registration Rules, 1925, substituted by the Land Registration (Capital Transfer Tax) Rules, 1975.) Accordingly if notice of an Inland Revenue charge is entered on the register, a purchaser should require a certificate of discharge (Form 61) just as with unregistered land.

PAGE
1171–
1180
contd. Also it should be noted that it is specially provided, in effect, that a purchaser will never become liable for tax in respect of objects of national, etc., importance, historic buildings and contents, timber and close company transactions (s. 26 (2)).

Incidence.—Not being of public revenue concern, the question of who bears the ultimate burden of capital transfer tax paid lacks any clear statutory statement. However, certain principles may be inferred, primarily from s. 28 of the Finance Act, 1975, which is directed to the methods of recovery of tax paid in various situations (with interest and costs : subs. (8)).

(a) *Gifts inter vivos.*—Practically, the donor/transferor should decide whether he or the donee/transferee is to bear the tax liability and arrange, through undertakings if necessary, that effect is given to his decision. This decision should, of course, be taken in the light of the " grossing-up " effect already mentioned (see s. 20 (2) and Sched. 10, para. 1 (2)). In the absence of any such decision or arrangements, it appears to be assumed throughout the legislation that the donor/transferor has no right to pass on his liability to the tax (see especially the terms of Sched. 10, para. 1 (2) (b)). In contrast provision is made whereby anyone else might recoup any liability for the tax as follows (s. 28 (3)) :

" Where a person is liable, otherwise than as transferor . . . for tax attributable to the value of any property he shall, for the purpose of paying the tax or raising the amount of it when paid, have power, whether or not the property is vested in him, to raise the amount of the tax by sale or mortgage of, or a terminable charge on, that property or any part thereof."

Presumably the intent was that the power of sale, etc., should be over the property transferred but again it has to be noted that the tax is attributable to the value of all the donor's property (ss. 20 (2), 23 (1)). Beyond this, recovery of the tax paid, e.g., by a successor in title to land who took subject to an Inland Revenue charge, becomes a matter of general law (especially no doubt of the covenants for title).

(b) *Transfer on death.*—In general, the liability to pay the tax falls on the personal representatives (see s. 25 (5) (a), above). Then the ultimate burden depends on whether or not an Inland Revenue charge arises (see Sched. 4, para. 20, above). If such a charge is imposed on any property, it is provided that the tax paid by the personal representatives " shall, where occasion requires, be repaid to them by the person in whom the property is vested " (s. 28 (1)). The combination of this blunt provision and of the imposition of the charge no doubt signifies that the tax will be borne by the beneficiaries taking the property, and if more than one according to their respective interests (i.e., as with an estate duty charge under s. 9 (1) of the Finance Act, 1894 : *Re Orford* [1896] 1 Ch. 257 ; and see s. 35 of the Administration of

PAGE
1171–
1180
contd.

Estates Act, 1925). The reference to "where occasion requires" must be taken as allowing for "free of duty" clauses to vary the incidence as with estate duty (and see s. 49 (5) as to existing free of duty clauses applying to capital transfer tax).

If no charge to capital transfer tax arises then it appears that the tax paid must be regarded as a testamentary expense, as was estate duty in similar cases (*Re Clemow* [1900] 2 Ch. 182 ; *Re Buesst's Will Trusts* [1963] Ch. 419). Accordingly, the incidence of the tax will be governed in the normal way by the order of application of assets set out in the Administration of Estates Act, 1925, s. 34 (3) and Sched. 1, Pt. II, which may be varied.

(c) *Other cases of charge.*—In other cases where capital transfer tax is paid, particularly in respect of settled property, the inference seems to be that the ultimate burden falls on capital and that the beneficial interests in both income and capital will consequently share the burden appropriately. Thus, s. 28 (3) quoted above is available generally, not just where there has been a gift *inter vivos*. Also subss. (4) and (5) of s. 28 enable the burden to be passed on to the capital of trust funds :

" (4) A person having a limited interest in any property who pays the tax attributable to the value of that property shall be entitled to the like charge as if the tax so attributable had been raised by means of a mortgage to him.

(5) Any money held on the trusts of a settlement may be expended in paying the tax attributable to the value of any property comprised in the settlement and held on the same trusts."

Accordingly the like questions of apportionment to those occurring with estate duty will occur here too.

(d) *Certificate.*—Provision is made for a person who has " paid or borne . . . tax for which he is not ultimately liable " to obtain a certificate from the Inland Revenue " specifying the tax paid and the debts and incumbrances allowed in valuing the property " (s. 28 (6)). This certificate, which seems to involve potentially difficult questions of fact and of law, is to be " conclusive as between any person by whom the tax specified in the certificate falls to be borne and the person seeking to recover the tax from him " (s. 28 (7) ; production of the certificate also suffices for any repayment of tax by the Inland Revenue).

Payment of tax by instalments.—Where capital transfer tax is attributable to the value of, *inter alia*, " land of any description, wherever situated " and the chargeable transfer was, generally, either on death or else *inter vivos* but with the donee bearing the tax, then there is an option to pay the tax by equal instalments yearly or half-yearly over eight years with interest (Sched. 4, para. 13, also

PAGE
1171–
1180
contd.

applying in some situations to settled property). This instalment option is made available also in respect of reimbursements of tax paid (s. 28 (2)). Despite exercise of the option, the whole balance of the tax may be paid at any time and also becomes payable immediately if the property is sold (Sched. 4, para. 13 (4)). If the option was exercised following an initial gift *inter vivos*, then immediate payment additionally becomes due on a subsequent gift *inter vivos* (*ibid.*, sub-para. (6) (*d*)). See also note against pp. 297–298 of main text.

Interest.—Capital transfer tax remaining unpaid, in effect, by the following April or within six months, whichever is longer, from the chargeable transfer, carries interest at 6 per cent. p.a. for a transfer on death but otherwise at 9 per cent. p.a. (Sched. 4, para. 19 (1)). Where payment is allowed by instalments the interest will only be in respect of any instalments not duly paid (Sched. 4, para. 13 (1)). Such interest is not deductible in computing any income, profits or losses for any tax purposes (Sched. 4, para. 19 (4)). Repayments of overpaid tax carry interest at the same rates from the date of payment which is not to be treated as income for tax purposes (Sched. 4, para. 19 (3), (4))—deliberate overpayment could therefore be considered a good investment : 9 per cent. p.a. tax-free !

Agricultural relief.—Subject to various complex conditions, there is still provision for relief for agricultural property (Sched. 8 to the 1975 Act). Assuming these conditions are fulfilled, the result is not a comparatively simple reduction in rate of tax as for estate duty but (*ibid.*, para. 2) :

> " Where the value transferred is to be computed in accordance with this paragraph there shall first be ascertained such part of the unreduced value as is attributable to the agricultural value of the agricultural property (in this Part of this Schedule referred to as the part eligible for relief) and the value transferred shall then be computed as if the part eligible for relief were reduced by applying to it the fraction of which—
>
> (*a*) the numerator is the multiplied rental value of the agricultural property ; and
>
> (*b*) the denominator is the agricultural value of the agricultural property."

Timber, etc.—Again there are various conditions, but some relief is still available under the misleading heading " Relief for Woodlands " (Sched. 9 to 1975 Act). This relief is only applicable in respect of a transfer on death and must be elected for within two years. It takes the form of leaving out of account " the value of the trees or underwood " (*not* of the land itself) but of imposing a charge on a later disposition thereof. Then the tax may be paid by instalments over eight years (Sched. 4, para. 15).

1182   *Third paragraph.*—Reference should also be made to *De Mulder* v. *Secretary of State for the Environment* [1974] Q.B. 792, where three enforcement notices relating to different parts of one planning unit were held to be unacceptable as a matter of law.

PAGE
1185 *Second paragraph.—Heron Service Stations, Ltd.* v. *Coupe* is reported at [1973] 1 W.L.R. 502.

1188 *Second paragraph.—Norfolk C.C.* v. *Secretary of State for the Environment* is reported at [1973] 1 W.L.R. 1400.

1189– **Development for which permission unnecessary.**—Attention
1190 should be drawn to subs. (1) of s. 23 of the 1971 Act, which provides that if an enforcement notice is served so that the present activity has to be discontinued, then " planning permission is not required for the use of that land for the purpose for which . . . it could lawfully have been used if that development had not been carried out." Thus the land owner or occupier has a right to revert to his former activity, even though this was a use without planning permission, if it had become established before 1968 (*LTSS Print and Supply Services, Ltd.* v. *Hackney London B.C.* [1975] 1 W.L.R. 138). Where the former use was commenced after 1963 (and so is not itself an established use : see main text at pp. 1188–89), although it may be resumed without planning permission for the resumption under s. 23 (9), contradictorily a planning authority may still serve an enforcement notice requiring its discontinuance (*W. T. Lamb & Sons, Ltd.* v. *Secretary of State for the Environment* [1975] 2 All E.R. 1117).

1191 *First paragraph.—Wood* v. *Secretary of State for the Environment* is reported at [1973] 1 W.L.R. 707.

1194 **Determination of applications.**—The question has arisen of the position where multiple, possibly inconsistent, permissions are granted and applied for in respect of the same land. In *Pilkington* v. *Secretary of State for the Environment* [1974] 1 All E.R. 283, at pp. 286–287, Lord Widgery, C. J., observed :

" There is, perhaps surprisingly, not very much authority on this point which one would think could often arise in practice, so I venture to start at the beginning with the more elementary principles which arise. In the first place I have no doubt that a landowner is entitled to make any number of applications for planning permission which his fancy dictates, even though the development referred to is quite different when one compares one application to another. It is open to a landowner to test the market by putting in a number of applications and seeing what the attitude of the planning authority is to his proposals.

Equally it seems to me that a planning authority receiving a number of planning applications in respect of the same land is required to deal with them, and to deal with them even though they are mutually inconsistent one with the other. Of course, special cases will arise where one application deliberately and expressly refers to or incorporates another, but we are not concerned with that type of application in the present case.

In the absence of any such complication, I would regard it as the duty of the planning authority to regard each application as a proposal in itself, and to apply its mind to each application, asking

PAGE
1194
contd.
itself whether the proposal there contained is consistent with good planning in the factual background against which the application is made.

I do not regard it as part of the duty of the local authority itself to relate one planning application or one planning permission to another to see if they are contradictory. Indeed I think it would be unnecessary officiousness if a planning authority did such a thing. They should regard each application as a proposal for a separate and independent development, and they should consider the merits of the application on that basis.''

See further the note against p. 1196.

1195   *First paragraph.—J. Murphy & Sons, Ltd.* v. *Secretary of State for the Environment* is reported at [1973] 1 W.L.R. 560.

1195   *Last paragraph* and

1196   *First paragraph.*—In *Kingston-upon-Thames Royal London B.C.* v. *Secretary of State for the Environment* [1974] 1 All E.R. 193 it was held to be an untenable proposition that a condition imposed on the grant of a planning permission cannot, unless compensation be paid, restrict existing activities which would be legal under planning law if the proposed development had not taken place. The condition in question, in effect held valid, restricted to car parking purposes the use of part of the land which was already lawfully used for other purposes.

1196   *Second paragraph.*—In *R.* v. *Hillingdon London B.C.* [1974] Q.B. 720, outline planning permission for building dwelling-houses had been granted subject to the conditions, *inter alia*, that the houses should be occupied by people on the authority's housing list with security of tenure for ten years. It was held that these conditions were clearly *ultra vires* since the authority sought to impose on the citizen performance of its own statutory duty. Further, the conditions were fundamental to the planning permission, which was also therefore void.

1196   **Construction of permission.**—Attention should be drawn to the need to construe a planning permission in the light of any other permissions relating to the same land, since after one permission has been implemented it will not be open to the landowner to implement another inconsistent permission : *Pilkington* v. *Secretary of State for the Environment* [1974] 1 All E.R. 283. An example given was as to different sites for a dwelling-house on one acre of land : they cannot all be built on. Lord Widgery, C.J., observed (at pp. 287–288) :

"It is said in the course of argument that any such decision is unfair to future purchasers. It is said that this decision as to the effect of conflicting planning permissions may operate to the detriment of a future purchaser who buys land and finds there is some shadow over it from some other permission which he was unaware of at the time of purchasing. I am unimpressed with this argument because an intended purchaser who is interested in

PAGE
1196
contd.
permissions affecting the land can find out by looking at the proper register ; if he looks at the register the position will be clear to him when he buys. If he does not look at the register he is no doubt content to take the land and take whatever planning permission he can persuade the local authority to grant."

1196–
1197
Appeals to the Secretary of State.—It has been held that the procedure of the prerogative orders is available in appropriate cases in respect of a planning authority exercising its jurisdictions under the Town and Country Planning Acts as an alternative to the appeals system established by these Acts : *R.* v. *Hillingdon London B.C.* [1974] Q.B. 720. In particular it will be proper to proceed by certiorari " where the decision in question is liable to be upset as a matter of law because on its face it is clearly made without jurisdiction or in consequence of an error of law " (*per* Lord Widgery, C.J., at p. 729, adding that this procedure would then be " more efficient, cheaper, and quicker ").

APPENDIX

AD VALOREM STAMP DUTY TABLES

1. Conveyances on sale: instruments executed on or after 1st May, 1974*

An instrument certified at £15,000 is not chargeable with any duty, but requires a " Produced " stamp.

Consideration not exceeding	Certificate of value £20,000	Certificate of value £25,000	Certificate of value £30,000	No Certificate of value
£	£	£	£	£
5	0·05	0·05	0·10	0·10
10	0·05	0·10	0·15	0·20
20	0·10	0·20	0·30	0·40
30	0·15	0·30	0·45	0·60
40	0·20	0·40	0·60	0·80
50	0·25	0·50	0·75	1·00
60	0·30	0·60	0·90	1·20
70	0·35	0·70	1·05	1·40
80	0·40	0·80	1·20	1·60
90	0·45	0·90	1·35	1·80
100	0·50	1·00	1·50	2·00
120	0·60	1·20	1·80	2·40
140	0·70	1·40	2·10	2·80
160	0·80	1·60	2·40	3·20
180	0·90	1·80	2·70	3·60
200	1·00	2·00	3·00	4·00
220	1·10	2·20	3·30	4·40
240	1·20	2·40	3·60	4·80
260	1·30	2·60	3·90	5·20
280	1·40	2·80	4·20	5·60
300	1·50	3·00	4·50	6·00
350	1·75	3·50	5·25	7·00
400	2·00	4·00	6·00	8·00
450	2·25	4·50	6·75	9·00
500	2·50	5·00	7·50	10·00
550	2·75	5·50	8·25	11·00
600	3·00	6·00	9·00	12·00
650	3·25	6·50	9·75	13·00
700	3·50	7·00	10·50	14·00
750	3·75	7·50	11·25	15·00
800	4·00	8·00	12·00	16·00
850	4·25	8·50	12·75	17·00
900	4·50	9·00	13·50	18·00
950	4·75	9·50	14·25	19·00
1,000	5·00	10·00	15·00	20·00
1,050	5·25	10·50	15·75	21·00
1,100	5·50	11·00	16·50	22·00
1,150	5·75	11·50	17·25	23·00
1,200	6·00	12·00	18·00	24·00
1,250	6·25	12·50	18·75	25·00
1,300	6·50	13·00	19·50	26·00
1,350	6·75	13·50	20·25	27·00
1,400	7·00	14·00	21·00	28·00
1,450	7·25	14·50	21·75	29·00

*Instruments executed in favour of charities on or after 1st August, 1974, if adjudicated, will not be liable to these rates but will remain subject to the rates in force immediately before 1st May, 1974 (F.A. 1974, s. 49 (2), (3)).

Consideration not exceeding	Certificate of value £20,000	Certificate of value £25,000	Certificate of value £30,000	No Certificate of value
£	£	£	£	£
1,500	7·50	15·00	22·50	30·00
1,550	7·75	15·50	23·25	31·00
1,600	8·00	16·00	24·00	32·00
1,650	8·25	16·50	24·75	33·00
1,700	8·50	17·00	25·50	34·00
1,750	8·75	17·50	26·25	35·00
1,800	9·00	18·00	27·00	36·00
1,850	9·25	18·50	27·75	37·00
1,900	9·50	19·00	28·50	38·00
1,950	9·75	19·50	29·25	39·00
2,000	10·00	20·00	30·00	40·00
2,050	10·25	20·50	30·75	41·00
2,100	10·50	21·00	31·50	42·00
2,150	10·75	21·50	32·25	43·00
2,200	11·00	22·00	33·00	44·00
2,250	11·25	22·50	33·75	45·00
2,300	11·50	23·00	34·50	46·00
2,350	11·75	23·50	35·25	47·00
2,400	12·00	24·00	36·00	48·00
2,450	12·25	24·50	36·75	49·00
2,500	12·50	25·00	37·50	50·00
2,550	12·75	25·50	38·25	51·00
2,600	13·00	26·00	39·00	52·00
2,650	13·25	26·50	39·75	53·00
2,700	13·50	27·00	40·50	54·00
2,750	13·75	27·50	41·25	55·00
2,800	14·00	28·00	42·00	56·00
2,850	14·25	28·50	42·75	57·00
2,900	14·50	29·00	43·50	58·00
2,950	14·75	29·50	44·25	59·00
3,000	15·00	30·00	45·00	60·00
3,050	15·25	30·50	45·75	61·00
3,100	15·50	31·00	46·50	62·00
3,150	15·75	31·50	47·25	63·00
3,200	16·00	32·00	48·00	64·00
3,250	16·25	32·50	48·75	65·00
3,300	16·50	33·00	49·50	66·00
3,350	16·75	33·50	50·25	67·00
3,400	17·00	34·00	51·00	68·00
3,450	17·25	34·50	51·75	69·00
3,500	17·50	35·00	52·50	70·00
3,550	17·75	35·50	53·25	71·00
3,600	18·00	36·00	54·00	72·00
3,650	18·25	36·50	54·75	73·00
3,700	18·50	37·00	55·50	74·00
3,750	18·75	37·50	56·25	75·00
3,800	19·00	38·00	57·00	76·00
3,850	19·25	38·50	57·75	77·00
3,900	19·50	39·00	58·50	78·00
3,950	19·75	39·50	59·25	79·00
4,000	20·00	40·00	60·00	80·00
4,050	20·25	40·50	60·75	81·00
4,100	20·50	41·00	61·50	82·00
4,150	20·75	41·50	62·25	83·00
4,200	21·00	42·00	63·00	84·00
4,250	21·25	42·50	63·75	85·00
4,300	21·50	43·00	64·50	86·00
4,350	21·75	43·50	65·25	87·00
4,400	22·00	44·00	66·00	88·00
4,450	22·25	44·50	66·75	89·00
4,500	22·50	45·00	67·50	90·00

Consideration not exceeding	Certificate of value £20,000	Certificate of value £25,000	Certificate of value £30,000	No Certificate of value
£	£	£	£	£
4,550	22·75	45·50	68·25	91·00
4,600	23·00	46·00	69·00	92·00
4,650	23·25	46·50	69·75	93·00
4,700	23·50	47·00	70·50	94·00
4,750	23·75	47·50	71·25	95·00
4,800	24·00	48·00	72·00	96·00
4,850	24·25	48·50	72·75	97·00
4,900	24·50	49·00	73·50	98·00
4,950	24·75	49·50	74·25	99·00
5,000	25·00	50·00	75·00	100·00
5,050	25·25	50·50	75·75	101·00
5,100	25·50	51·00	76·50	102·00
5,150	25·75	51·50	77·25	103·00
5,200	26·00	52·00	78·00	104·00
5,250	26·25	52·50	78·75	105·00
5,300	26·50	53·00	79·50	106·00
5,350	26·75	53·50	80·25	107·00
5,400	27·00	54·00	81·00	108·00
5,450	27·25	54·50	81·75	109·00
5,500	27·50	55·00	82·50	110·00
5,550	27·75	55·50	83·25	111·00
5,600	28·00	56·00	84·00	112·00
5,650	28·25	56·50	84·75	113·00
5,700	28·50	57·00	85·50	114·00
5,750	28·75	57·50	86·25	115·00
5,800	29·00	58·00	87·00	116·00
5,850	29·25	58·50	87·75	117·00
5,900	29·50	59·00	88·50	118·00
5,950	29·75	59·50	89·25	119·00
6,000	30·00	60·00	90·00	120·00
6,050	30·25	60·50	90·75	121·00
6,100	30·50	61·00	91·50	122·00
6,150	30·75	61·50	92·25	123·00
6,200	31·00	62·00	93·00	124·00
6,250	31·25	62·50	93·75	125·00
6,300	31·50	63·00	94·50	126·00
6,350	31·75	63·50	95·25	127·00
6,400	32·00	64·00	96·00	128·00
6,450	32·25	64·50	96·75	129·00
6,500	32·50	65·00	97·50	130·00
6,550	32·75	65·50	98·25	131·00
6,600	33·00	66·00	99·00	132·00
6,650	33·25	66·50	99·75	133·00
6,700	33·50	67·00	100·50	134·00
6,750	33·75	67·50	101·25	135·00
6,800	34·00	68·00	102·00	136·00
6,850	34·25	68·50	102·75	137·00
6,900	34·50	69·00	103·50	138·00
6,950	34·75	69·50	104·24	139·00
7,000	35·00	70·00	105·00	140·00
7,050	35·25	70·50	105·75	141·00
7,100	35·50	71·00	106·50	142·00
7,150	35·75	71·50	107·25	143·00
7,200	36·00	72·00	108·00	144·00
7,250	36·25	72·50	108·75	145·00
7,300	36·50	73·00	109·50	146·00
7,350	36·75	73·50	110·25	147·00
7,400	37·00	74·00	111·00	148·00
7,450	37·25	74·50	111·75	149·00
7,500	37·50	75·00	112·50	150·00
7,550	37·75	75·50	113·25	151·00

Consideration not exceeding	Certificate of value £20,000	Certificate of value £25,000	Certificate of value £30,000	No Certificate of value
£	£	£	£	£
7,600	38·00	76·00	114·00	152·00
7,650	38·25	76·50	114·75	153·00
7,700	38·50	77·00	115·50	154·00
7,750	38·75	77·50	116·25	155·00
7,800	39·00	78·00	117·00	156·00
7,850	39·25	78·50	117·75	157·00
7,900	39·50	79·00	118·50	158·00
7,950	39·75	79·50	119·25	159·00
8,000	40·00	80·00	120·00	160·00
8,050	40·25	80·50	120·75	161·00
8,100	40·50	81·00	121·50	162·00
8,150	40·75	81·50	122·25	163·00
8,200	41·00	82·00	123·00	164·00
8,250	41·25	82·50	123·75	165·00
8,300	41·50	83·00	124·50	166·00
8,350	41·75	83·50	125·25	167·00
8,400	42·00	84·00	126·00	168·00
8,450	42·25	84·50	126·75	169·00
8,500	52·50	85·00	127·50	170·00
8,550	42·75	85·50	128·25	171·00
8,600	43·00	86·00	129·00	172·00
8,650	43·25	86·50	129·75	173·00
8,700	43·50	87·00	130·50	174·00
8,750	43·75	87·50	131·25	175·00
8,800	44·00	88·00	132·00	176·00
8,850	44·25	88·50	132·75	177·00
8,900	44·50	89·00	133·50	178·00
8,950	44·75	89·50	134·25	179·00
9,000	45·00	90·00	135·00	180·00
9,050	45·25	90·50	135·75	181·00
9,100	45·50	91·00	136·50	182·00
9,150	45·75	91·50	137·25	183·00
9,200	46·00	92·00	138·00	184·00
9,250	46·25	92·50	138·75	185·00
9,300	46·50	93·00	139·50	186·00
9,350	46·75	93·50	140·25	187·00
9,400	47·00	94·00	141·00	188·00
9,450	46·25	94·50	141·75	189·00
9,500	47·50	95·00	142·50	190·00
9,550	47·75	95·50	143·25	191·00
9,600	48·00	96·00	144·00	192·00
9,650	48·25	96·50	144·75	193·00
9,700	48·50	97·00	145·50	194·00
9,750	48·75	97·50	146·25	195·00
9,800	49·00	98·00	147·00	196·00
9,850	49·25	98·50	147·75	197·00
9,900	49·50	99·00	148·50	198·00
9,950	49·75	99·50	149·25	199·00
10,000	50·00	100·00	150·00	200·00
10,050	50·25	100·50	150·75	201·00
10,100	50·50	101·00	151·50	202·00
10,150	50·75	101·50	152·25	203·00
10,200	51·00	102·00	153·00	204·00
10,250	51·25	102·50	153·75	205·00
10,300	51·50	103·00	154·50	206·00
10,350	51·75	103·50	155·25	207·00
10,400	52·00	104·00	156·00	208·00
10,450	52·25	104·50	156·75	209·00
10,500	52·50	105·00	157·50	210·00
10,550	52·75	105·50	158·25	211·00
10,600	53·00	106·00	159·00	212·00

Consideration not exceeding	Certificate of value £20,000	Certificate of value £25,000	Certificate of value £30,000	No Certificate of value
£	£	£	£	£
10,650	53·25	106·50	159·75	213·00
10,700	53·50	107·00	160·50	214·00
10,750	53·75	107·50	161·25	215·00
10,800	54·00	108·00	162·00	216·00
10,850	54·25	108·50	162·75	217·00
10,900	54·50	109·00	163·50	218·00
10,950	54·75	109·50	164·25	219·00
11,000	55·00	110·00	165·00	220·00
11,050	55·25	110·50	165·75	221·00
11,100	55·50	111·00	166·50	222·00
11,150	55·75	111·50	167·25	223·00
11,200	56·00	112·00	168·00	224·00
11,250	56·25	112·50	168·75	225·00
11,300	56·50	113·00	169·50	226·00
11,350	56·75	113·50	170·25	227·00
11,400	57·00	114·00	171·00	228·00
11,450	57·25	114·50	171·75	229·00
11,500	57·50	115·00	172·50	230·00
11,550	57·75	115·50	173·25	231·00
11,600	58·00	116·00	174·00	232·00
11,650	58·25	116·50	174·75	233·00
11,700	58·50	117·00	175·50	234·00
11,750	58·75	117·50	176·25	235·00
11,800	59·00	118·00	177·00	236·00
11,850	59·25	118·50	177·75	237·00
11,900	59·50	119·00	178·50	238·00
11,950	59·75	119·50	179·25	239·00
12,000	60·00	120·00	180·00	240·00
12,050	60·25	120·50	180·75	241·00
12,100	60·50	121·00	181·50	242·00
12,150	60·75	121·50	182·25	243·00
12,200	61·00	122·00	183·00	244·00
12,250	61·25	122·50	183·75	245·00
12,300	61·50	123·00	184·50	246·00
12,350	61·75	123·50	185·25	247·00
12,400	62·00	124·00	186·00	248·00
12,450	62·25	124·50	186·75	249·00
12,500	62·50	125·00	187·50	250·00
12,550	62·75	125·50	188·25	251·00
12,600	63·00	126·00	189·00	252·00
12,650	63·25	126·50	189·75	253·00
12,700	63·50	127·00	190·50	254·00
12,750	63·75	127·50	191·25	255·00
12,800	64·00	128·00	192·00	256·00
12,850	64·25	128·50	192·75	257·00
12,900	64·50	129·00	193·50	258·00
12,950	64·75	129·50	194·25	259·00
13,000	65·00	130·00	195·00	260·00
13,050	65·25	130·50	195·75	261·00
13,100	65·50	131·00	196·50	262·00
13,150	65·75	131·50	197·25	263·00
13,200	66·00	132·00	198·00	264·00
13,250	66·25	132·50	198·75	265·00
13,300	66·50	133·00	199·50	266·00
13,350	66·75	133·50	200·25	267·00
13,400	67·00	134·00	201·00	268·00
13,450	67·25	134·50	201·75	269·00
13,500	67·50	135·00	202·50	270·00
13,550	67·75	135·50	203·25	271·00
13,600	68·00	136·00	204·00	272·00
13,650	68·25	136·50	204·75	273·00

9

Consideration not exceeding	Certificate of value £20,000	Certificate of value £25,000	Certificate of value £30,000	No Certificate of value
£	£	£	£	£
13,700	68·50	137·00	205·50	274·00
13,750	68·75	137·50	206·25	275·00
13,800	69·00	138·00	207·00	276·00
13,850	69·25	138·50	207·75	277·00
13,900	69·50	139·00	208·50	278·00
13,950	69·75	139·50	209·25	279·00
14,000	70·00	140·00	210·00	280·00
14,050	70·25	140·50	210·75	281·00
14,100	70·50	141·00	211·50	282·00
14,150	70·75	141·50	212·25	283·00
14,200	71·00	142·00	213·00	284·00
14,250	71·25	142·50	213·75	285·00
14,300	71·50	143·00	214·50	286·00
14,350	71·75	143·50	215·25	287·00
14,400	72·00	144·00	216·00	288·00
14,450	72·25	144·50	216·75	289·00
14,500	72·50	145·00	217·50	290·00
14,550	72·75	145·50	218·25	291·00
14,600	73·00	146·00	219·00	292·00
14,650	73·25	146·50	219·75	293·00
14,700	73·50	147·00	220·50	294·00
14,750	73·75	147·50	221·25	295·00
14,800	74·00	148·00	222·00	296·00
14,850	74·25	148·50	222·75	297·00
14,900	74·50	149·00	223·50	298·00
14,950	74·75	149·50	224·25	299·00
15,000	75·00	150·00	225·00	300·00
15,050	75·25	150·50	225·75	301·00
15,100	75·50	151·00	226·50	302·00
15,150	75·75	151·50	227·25	303·00
15,200	76·00	152·00	228·00	304·00
15,250	76·25	152·50	228·75	305·00
15,300	76·50	153·00	229·50	306·00
15,350	76·75	153·50	230·25	307·00
15,400	77·00	154·00	231·00	308·00
15,450	77·25	154·50	231·75	309·00
15,500	77·50	155·00	232·50	310·00
15,550	77·75	155·50	233·25	211·00
15,600	78·00	156·00	234·00	312·00
15,650	78·25	156·50	234·75	313·00
15,700	78·50	157·00	235·50	314·00
15,750	78·75	157·50	236·25	315·00
15,800	79·00	158·00	237·00	316·00
15,850	79·25	158·50	237·75	317·00
15,900	79·50	159·00	238·50	318·00
15,950	79·75	159·50	239·25	319·00
16,000	80·00	160·00	240·00	320·00
16,050	80·25	160·50	240·75	321·00
16,100	80·50	161·00	241·50	322·00
16,150	80·75	161·50	242·25	323·00
16,200	81·00	162·00	243·00	324·00
16,250	81·25	162·50	243·75	325·00
16,300	81·50	163·00	244·50	326·00
16,350	81·75	163·50	245·25	327·00
16,400	82·00	164·00	246·00	328·00
16,450	82·25	164·50	246·75	329·00
16,500	82·50	165·00	247·50	330·00
16,550	82·75	165·50	248·25	331·00
16,600	83·00	166·00	249·00	332·00
16,650	83·25	166·50	249·75	333·00
16,700	83·50	167·00	250·50	334·00

Consideration not exceeding	Certificate of value £20,000	Certificate of value £25,000	Certificate of value £30,000	No Certificate of value
£	£	£	£	£
16,750	83·75	167·50	251·25	335·00
16,800	84·00	168·00	252·00	336·00
16,850	84·25	168·50	252·75	337·00
16,900	84·50	169·00	253·50	338·00
16,950	84·75	169·50	254·25	339·00
17,000	85·00	170·00	255·00	340·00
17,050	85·25	170·50	255·75	341·00
17,100	85·50	171·00	256·50	342·00
17,150	85·75	171·50	257·25	343·00
17,200	86·00	172·00	258·00	344·00
17,250	86·25	172·50	258·75	345·00
17,300	86·50	173·00	259·50	346·00
17,350	86·75	173·50	260·25	347·00
17,400	87·00	174·00	261·00	348·00
17,450	87·25	174·50	261·75	349·00
17,500	87·50	175·00	262·50	350·00
17,750	87·75	175·50	263·25	351·00
17,600	88·00	176·00	264·00	352·00
17,650	88·25	176·50	264·75	353·00
17,700	88·50	177·00	265·50	354·00
17,750	88·75	177·50	266·25	355·00
17,800	89·00	178·00	267·00	356·00
17,850	89·25	178·50	267·75	357·00
17,900	89·50	179·00	268·50	358·00
17,950	89·75	179·50	269·25	359·00
18,000	90·00	180·00	270·00	360·00
18,050	90·25	180·50	270·75	361·00
18,100	90·50	181·00	271·50	362·00
18,150	90·75	181·50	272·25	363·00
18,200	91·00	182·00	273·00	364·00
18,250	91·25	182·50	273·75	365·00
18,300	91·50	183·00	274·50	366·00
18,350	91·75	183·50	275·25	367·00
18,400	92·00	184·00	276·00	368·00
18,450	92·25	184·50	276·75	369·00
18,500	92·50	185·00	277·50	370·00
18,550	92·75	185·50	278·25	371·00
18,600	93·00	186·00	279·00	372·00
18,650	93·25	186·50	279·75	373·00
18,700	93·50	187·00	280·50	374·00
18,750	93·75	187·50	281·25	375·00
18,800	94·00	188·00	282·00	376·00
18,850	94·25	188·50	282·75	377·00
18,900	94·50	189·00	283·50	378·00
18,950	94·75	189·50	284·25	379·00
19,000	95·00	190·00	285·00	380·00
19,050	95·25	190·50	285·75	381·00
19,100	95·50	191·00	286·50	382·00
19,150	95·75	191·50	287·25	383·00
19,200	96·00	192·00	288·00	384·00
19,250	96·25	192·50	288·75	385·00
19,300	96·50	193·00	289·50	386·00
19,350	96·75	193·50	290·25	387·00
19,400	97·00	194·00	291·00	388·00
19,450	97·25	194·50	291·75	389·00
19,500	97·50	195·00	292·50	390·00
19,550	97·75	195·50	293·25	391·00
19,600	98·00	196·00	294·00	392·00
19,650	98·25	196·50	294·75	393·00
19,700	98·50	197·00	295·50	394·00
19,750	98·75	197·50	296·25	395·00

Consideration not exceeding	Certificate of value £20,000	Certificate of value £25,000	Certificate of value £30,000	No Certificate of value
£	£	£	£	£
19,800	99·00	198·00	297·00	396·00
19,850	99·25	198·50	297·75	397·00
19,900	99·50	199·00	298·50	398·00
19,950	99·75	199·50	299·25	399·00
20,000	100·00	200·00	300·00	400·00
20,050		200·50	300·75	401·00
20,100		201·00	301·50	402·00
20,150		201·50	302·25	403·00
20,200		202·00	303·00	404·00
20,250		202·50	303·75	405·00
20,300		203·00	304·50	406·00
20,350		203·50	305·25	407·00
20,400		204·00	306·00	408·00
20,450		204·50	306·75	409·00
20,500		205·00	307·50	410·00
20,550		205·50	308·25	411·00
20,600		206·00	309·00	412·00
20,650		206·50	309·75	413·00
20,700		207·00	310·50	414·00
20,750		207·50	311·25	415·00
20,800		208·00	312·00	416·00
20,850		208·50	312·75	417·00
20,900		209·00	313·50	418·00
20,950		209·50	314·25	419·00
21,000		210·00	315·00	420·00
21,050		210·50	315·75	421·00
21,100		211·00	316·50	422·00
21,150		211·50	317·25	423·00
21,200		212·00	318·00	424·00
21,250		212·50	318·75	425·00
21,300		213·00	319·50	426·00
21,350		213·50	320·25	427·00
21,400		214·00	321·00	428·00
21,450		214·50	321·75	429·00
21,500		215·00	322·50	430·00
21,550		215·50	323·25	431·00
21,600		216·00	324·00	432·00
21,650		216·50	324·75	433·00
21,700		217,00	325·50	434·00
21,750		217·50	326·25	435·00
21,800		218·00	327·00	436·00
21,850		218·50	327·75	437·00
21,900		219·00	328·50	438·00
21,950		219·50	329·25	439·00
22,000		220·00	330·00	440·00
22,050		220·50	330·75	441·00
22,100		221·00	331·50	442·00
22,150		221·50	332·25	443·00
22,200		222·00	333·00	444·00
22,250		222·50	333·75	445·00
22,300		223·00	334·50	446·00
22,350		223·50	335·25	447·00
22,400		224·00	336·00	448·00
22,450		224·50	336·75	449·00
22,500		225·00	337·50	450·00
22,550		225·50	338·25	451·00
22,600		226·00	339·00	452·00
22,650		226·50	339·75	453·00
22,700		227·00	340·50	454·00
22,750		227·50	341·25	455·00
22,800		228·00	342·00	456·00

Consideration not exceeding	Certificate of value £20,000	Certificate of value £25,000	Certificate of value £30,000	No Certificate of value
£	£	£	£	£
22,850		228·50	342·75	457·00
22,900		229·00	343·50	458·00
22,950		229·50	344·25	459·00
23,000		230·00	345·00	460·00
23,050		230·50	345·75	461·00
23,100		231·00	346·50	462·00
23,150		231·50	347·25	463·00
23,200		232·00	348·00	464·00
23,250		232·50	348·75	465·00
23,300		233·00	349·50	466·00
23,350		233·50	350·25	467·00
23,400		234·00	351·00	468·00
23,450		234·50	351·75	469·00
23,500		235·00	352·50	470·00
23,550		235·50	353·25	471·00
23,600		236·00	354·00	472·00
23,650		236·50	354·75	473·00
23,700		237·00	355·50	474·00
23,750		237·50	356·25	475·00
23,800		238·00	357·00	476·00
23,850		238·50	357·75	477·00
23,900		239·00	358·50	478·00
23,950		239·50	359·25	479·00
24,000		240·00	360·00	480·00
24,050		240·50	360·75	481·00
24,100		241·00	361·50	482·00
24,150		241·50	362·25	483·00
24,200		242·00	363·00	484·00
24,250		242·50	363·75	485·00
24,300		243·00	364·50	486·00
24,350		243·50	365·25	487·00
24,400		244·00	366·00	488·00
24,450		244·50	366·75	489·00
24,500		245·00	367·50	490·00
24,550		245·50	368·25	491·00
24,600		246·00	369·00	492·00
24,650		246·50	369·75	493·00
24,700		247·00	370·50	494·00
24,750		247·50	371·25	495·00
24,800		248·00	372·00	496·00
24,850		248·50	372·75	497·00
24,900		249·00	373·50	498·00
24,950		249·50	374·25	499·00
25,000		250·00	375·00	500·00
25,050			375·75	501·00
25,100			376·50	502·00
25,150			377·25	503·00
25,200			378·00	504·00
25,250			378·75	505·00
25,300			379·50	506·00
25,350			380·25	507·00
25,400			381·00	508·00
25,450			381·75	509·00
25,500			382·50	510·00
25,550			383·25	511·00
25,600			384·00	512·00
25,650			384·75	513·00
25,700			385·50	514·00
25,750			386·25	515·00
25,800			387·00	516·00
25,850			387·75	517·00

Consideration not exceeding	Certificate of value £20,000	Certificate of value £25,000	Certificate of value £30,000	No Certificate of value
£	£	£	£	£
25,900			388·50	518·00
25,950			389·25	519·00
26,000			390·00	520·00
26,050			390·75	521·00
26,100			391·50	522·00
26,150			392·25	523·00
26,200			393·00	524·00
26,250			393·75	525·00
26,300			394·50	526·00
26,350			395·25	527·00
26,400			396·00	528·00
26,450			396·75	529·00
26,500			397·50	530·00
26,550			398·25	531·00
26,600			399·00	532·00
26,650			399·75	533·00
26,700			400·50	534·00
26,750			401·25	535·00
26,800			402·00	536·00
26,850			402·75	537·00
26,900			403·50	538·00
26,950			404·25	539·00
27,000			405·00	540·00
27,050			405·75	541·00
27,100			406·50	542·00
27,150			407·25	543·00
27,200			408·00	544·00
27,250			408·75	545·00
27,300			409·50	546·00
27,350			410·25	547·00
27,400			411·00	548·00
27,450			411·75	549·00
27,500			412·50	550·00
27,550			413·25	551·00
27,600			414·00	552·00
27,650			414·75	553·00
27,700			415·50	554·00
27,750			416·25	555·00
27,800			417·00	556·00
27,850			417·75	557·00
27,900			418·50	558·00
27,950			419·25	559·00
28,000			420·00	560·00
28,050			420·75	561·00
28,100			421·50	562·00
28,150			422·25	563·00
28,200			423·00	564·00
28,250			423·75	565·00
28,300			424·50	566·00
28,350			425·25	567·00
28,400			426·00	568·00
28,450			426·75	569·00
28,500			427·50	570·00
28,550			428·25	571·00
28,600			429·00	572·00
28,650			429·75	573·00
28,700			430·50	574·00
28,750			431·25	575·00
28,800			432·00	576·00
28,850			432·75	577·00
28,900			433·50	578·00

Consideration not exceeding	Certificate of value £20,000	Certificate of value £25,000	Certificate of value £30,000	No Certificate of value
£	£	£	£	£
28,950			434·25	579·00
29,000			435·00	580·00
29,050			435·75	581·00
29,100			436·50	582·00
29,150			437·25	583·00
29,200			438·00	584·00
29,250			438·75	585·00
29,300			439·50	586·00
29,350			440·25	587·00
29,400			441·00	588·00
29,450			441·75	589·00
29,500			442·50	590·00
29,550			443·25	591·00
29,600			444·00	592·00
29,650			444·75	593·00
29,700			445·50	594·00
29,750			446·25	595·00
29,800			447·00	596·00
29,850			447·75	597·00
29,900			448·50	598·00
29,950			449·25	599·00
30,000			450·00	600·00
Exceeding £30,000				£1 for every £50 or part of £50 of the total consideration

2. Instruments executed on or after 1st January, 1892, but before 1st May, 1974.

The table below shows the rates of duty applicable between 1st January, 1892, and 30th April, 1974, inclusive, according to the date of execution and whether any and if so what certificate of value* is included in the instrument. Duty is calculated at intervals of £50, except where the consideration is under £300 (see note † below).

Consideration £	DATE OF EXECUTION 1st January, 1892, to 28th April, 1910	29th April, 1910,* to 31st July, 1947	1st August, 1947, to 9th July, 1952	10th July, 1952, to 31st July, 1956
500 or under	£½%	C£500: £½% — No certificate: £½%	C£500: £½% — C£1,500: £1% — No certificate: £2%‡	C£500: £½% — C£3,000: £1% — C£3,450: £1½%‡ — No certificate: £2%‡
501–1,500	£½%	£1%	C£1,500: £1% — No certificate: £2%‡	C£3,000: £1% — C£3,450: £1½%‡ — No certificate: £2%‡
1,501–1,950	£½%	£1%	" Single transaction " certificate (F.A., 1947, s. 54 (3)): see note § — No certificate· £2%‡	(as above)
1,951–3,000	£½%	£1%	£2%‡	(as above)
3,001–3,450	£½%	£1%	£2%‡	C£3,450: £1½%‡ — No certificate: £2%‡
3,451–3,500	£½%	£1%	£2%‡	£2%‡
3,501–4,250	£½%	£1%	£2%‡	£2%‡
4,251–4,500	£½%	£1%	£2%‡	£2%‡
4,501–5,000	£½%	£1%	£2%‡	£2%‡
5,001–5,250	£½%	£1%	£2%‡	£2%‡
5,251–5,500	£½%	£1%	£2%‡	£2%
5,501–6,000	£½%	£1%	£2%‡	£2%‡
6,000–7,000	£½%	£1%	£2%‡	£2%‡
7,000–10,000	£½%	£1%	£2%‡	£2%‡
10,000–15,000	£½%	£1%	£2%‡	£2%‡
Over 15 000	£½%	£1%	£2%‡	£2%‡

*Certificates of value are denoted by the prefix C followed by the amount mentioned in the certificate in question (viz., £500: F. (1909–10) A., 1910, s. 73; (leases) Revenue Act, 1911, s. 15; £1,500: F.A., 1947, s. 54 (3); £3,000: F.A., 1952, s. 73; £3,450: F.A., 1952, s. 73; £3,500: F.A., 1956, s. 37, and F.A., 1958, s. 34; £4,250: F.A., 1956, s. 37; £4,500: F.A., 1958, s. 34, and F.A., 1963, s. 55; £5,000: F.A., 1956, s. 37; £5,250: F.A., 1958, s. 34; £5,500: F.A., 1967, s. 27; £6,000: F.A., 1958, s. 34, and F.A., 1963, s. 55; £7,000: F.A., 1967, s. 27; £10,000 or £15,000: F.A., 1972, s. 125). Note that the £500 certificate of value in relation to leases introduced by the Revenue Act, 1911, operated from 31st March, 1911.

†For amounts up to £300, duty is calculated at intervals of less than £50, viz.:—

(*a*) for instruments executed before 1st August, 1970, at £5 intervals up to £25, then at £25 intervals to £300; and if the consideration is less than £5 and the instrument is executed on or after 1st August, 1959, duty payable is limited to 6d. for every 25s. or part of 25s. of the consideration;

(*b*) for instruments executed on or after 1st August, 1970, at £10 intervals up to £100, then at £20 intervals to £300; and if the consideration does not exceed £5, duty is 1s.

DATE OF EXECUTION

1st August, 1956, to 31st July, 1958	1st August, 1958, to 31st July, 1963	1st August, 1963, to 31st July, 1967	1st August, 1967, to 31st July, 1972	1st August, 1972, to 30th April, 1974
C£3,500: £½% C£4,250: £1% C£5,000: £1½%‡ No certificate: £2%‡	C£3,500: Nil C£4,500: £1% C£5,250: £1% C£6,000: £1½%‡ No certificate: £2%‡	C£4,500: Nil C£6,000: £½% No certificate: £1%	C£5,500: Nil C£7,000: £¼% No certificate: £1%	C£10,000: Nil C£15,000: £¼% No certificate: £1%
(as above)	(as above)	(as above)	(as above)	(as above)
(as above)	(as above)	(as above)	(as above)	(as above)
(as above)	(as above)	(as above)	(as above)	(as above)
(as above)	(as above)	(as above)	(as above)	(as above)
(as above)	(as above)	(as above)	(as above)	(as above)
C£4,250: £1% C£5,000: £1½%‡ No certificate: £2%‡	C£4,500: £½% C£5,250: £1% C£6,000: £1½%‡ No certificate: £2%‡	(as above)	(as above)	(as above)
C£5,000: £1½%‡ No certificate: £2%‡	(as above)	(as above)	(as above)	(as above)
(as above)	C£5,250: £1% C£6,000: £1½%‡ No certificate: £2%‡	C£6,000: £¼% No certificate: £1%	(as above)	(as above)
£2%‡	(as above)	(as above)	(as above)	(as above)
£2%‡	C£6,000: £1½%‡ No certificate: £2%‡	(as above)	(as above)	(as above)
£2%‡	(as above)	(as above)	C£7,000: £½% No certificate: £½%	(as above)
£2%‡	£2%‡	£1%	(as above)	(as above)
£2%‡	£2%‡	£1%	£1%	(as above)
£2%‡	£2%‡	£1%	£1%	C£15,000: £½% No certificate: £1%
£2%‡	£2%‡	£1%	£1%	£1%

‡Not applicable to conveyances to charities, etc.—see F.A., 1947, s. 54, and F.A., 1958, s. 34 (6).

§Sliding scale applicable as follows:—

Consideration	£1,550	£1,600	£1,650	£1,700	£1,750
Duty (see note ‡ above) ..	£17 10s.	£20	£22 10s.	£25	£27 10s.
Consideration	£1,800	£1,850	£1,900	£1,950	
Duty (see note ‡ above) ..	£30	£32 10s.	£25	£37 10s.	

3. " Particulars Delivered " Stamp, etc.

Section 28 of the F.A. 1931, requiring production of instruments to the Commissioners within thirty days of execution, came into force on 1st September, 1931.

The " P.D." stamp was required on conveyances on sale and leases for a term exceeding fourteen years from 29th April, 1910, to 18th July, 1923 (F. (1909–10) A. 1910, s. 4 ; F.A. 1923, s. 38). Its absence from instruments dated after 3rd August, 1920, however, is not thought to be a defect in title (F.A. 1920, s. 57).

Conveyances of land purchased under statutory authority must be stamped as produced since 30th May, 1895 (F.A. 1895, s. 12).

4. Leases: instruments executed on or after 1st May, 1974

Rent not exceeding	TERM OF LEASE			
	Not exceeding 7 years or indefinite	Exceeding 7 years but not exceeding 35 years	Exceeding 35 years but not exceeding 100 years	Exceeding 100 years
£	£	£	£	£
5		0·10	0·60	1·20
10		0·20	1·20	2·40
15		0·30	1·80	3·60
20		0·40	2·40	4·80
25		0·50	3·00	6·00
50	NIL	1·00	6·00	12·00
75		1·50	9·00	18·00
100		2·00	12·00	24·00
150		3·00	18·00	36·00
200		4·00	24·00	48·00
250		5·00	30·00	60·00
300	3·00	6·00	36·00	72·00
350	3·50	7·00	42·00	84·00
400	4·00	8·00	48·00	96·00
450	4·50	9·00	54·00	108·00
500	5·00	10·00	60·00	120·00
550	5·50	11·00	66·00	132·00
600	6·00	12·00	72·00	144·00
650	6·50	13·00	78·00	156·00
700	7·00	14·00	84·00	168·00
750	7·50	15·00	90·00	180·00
800	8·00	16·00	96·00	192·00
850	8·50	17·00	102·00	204·00
900	9·00	18·00	108·00	216·00
950	9·50	19·00	114·00	228·00
1,000	10·00	20·00	120·00	240·00
1,050	10·50	21·00	126·00	252·00
1,100	11·00	22·00	132·00	264·00
1,150	11·50	23·00	138·00	276·00
1,200	12·00	24·00	144·00	288·00
1,250	12·50	25·00	150·00	300·00
1,300	13·00	26·00	156·00	312·00
1,350	13·50	27·00	162·00	324·00
1,400	14·00	28·00	168·00	336·00
1,450	14·50	29·00	174·00	348·00
1,500	15·00	30·00	180·00	360·00

Rent not exceeding	TERM OF LEASE			
	Not exceeding 7 years or indefinite	Exceeding 7 years but not exceeding 35 years	Exceeding 35 years but not exceeding 100 years	Exceeding 100 years
£	£	£	£	£
1,550	15·50	31·00	186·00	372·00
1,600	16·00	32·00	192·00	384·00
1,650	16·50	33·00	198·00	396·00
1,700	17·00	34·00	204·00	408·00
1,750	17·50	35·00	210·00	420·00
1,800	18·00	36·00	216·00	432·00
1,850	18·50	37·00	222·00	444·00
1,900	**19·00**	38·00	228·00	456·00
1,950	19·50	39·00	234·00	468·00
2,000	20·00	40·00	240·00	480·00
2,050	20·50	41·00	246·00	492·00
2,100	21·00	42·00	252·00	504·00
2,150	21·50	43·00	258·00	516·00
2,200	22·00	44·00	264·00	528·00
2,250	22·50	45·00	270·00	540·00
2,300	23·00	46·00	276·00	552·00
2,350	23·50	47·00	282·00	564·00
2,400	24·00	48·00	288·00	576·00
2,450	24·50	49·00	294·00	588·00
2,500	25·00	50·00	300·00	600·00
2,550	25·50	51·00	306·00	612·00
2,600	26·00	52·00	312·00	624·00
2,650	26·50	53·00	318·00	636·00
2,700	27·00	54·00	324·00	648·00
2,750	27·50	55·00	330·00	660·00
2,800	28·00	56·00	336·00	672·00
2,850	28·50	57·00	342·00	684·00
2,900	29·00	58·00	348·00	696·00
2,950	29·50	59·00	354·00	708·00
3,000	30·00	60·00	360·00	720·00
3,050	30·50	61·00	366·00	732·00
3,100	31·00	62·00	372·00	744·00
3,150	31·50	63·00	378·00	756·00
3,200	32·00	64·00	384·00	768·00
3,250	32·50	65·00	390·00	780·00
3,300	33·00	66·00	396·00	792·00
3,350	33·50	67·00	402·00	804·00
3,400	34·00	68·00	408·00	816·00
3,450	34·50	69·00	414·00	828·00
3,500	35·00	70·00	420·00	840·00
3,550	35·50	71·00	426·00	852·00
3,600	36·00	72·00	432·00	864·00
3,650	36·50	73·00	438·00	876·00
3,700	37·00	74·00	444·00	888·00
3,750	37·50	75·00	450·00	900·00
3,800	38·00	76·00	456·00	912·00
3,850	38·50	77·00	462·00	924·00
3,900	39·00	78·00	468·00	936·00
3,950	39·50	79·00	474·00	948·00
4,000	40·00	80·00	480·00	960·00
4,050	40·50	81·00	486·00	972·00
4,100	41·00	82·00	492·00	984·00
4,150	41·50	83·00	498·00	996·00
4,200	42·00	84·00	504·00	1008·00
4,250	42·50	85·00	510·00	1020·00
4,300	43·00	86·00	516·00	1032·00
4,350	43·50	87·00	522·00	1044·00
4,400	44·00	88·00	528·00	1056·00

Rent not exceeding	TERM OF LEASE			
	Not exceeding 7 years or indefinite	Exceeding 7 years but not exceeding 35 years	Exceeding 35 years but not exceeding 100 years	Exceeding 100 years
£	£	£	£	£
4,450	44·50	89·00	534·00	1068·00
4,500	45·00	90·00	540·00	1080·00
4,550	45·50	91·00	546·00	1092·00
4,600	46·00	92·00	552·00	1104·00
4,650	46·50	93·00	558·00	1116·00
4,700	47·00	94·00	564·00	1128·00
4,750	47·50	95·00	570·00	1140·00
4,800	48·00	96·00	576·00	1152·00
4,850	48·50	97·00	582·00	1164·00
4,900	49·00	98·00	588·00	1176·00
4,950	49·50	99·00	594·00	1188·00
5,000	50·00	100·00	600·00	1200·00
5,050	50·50	101·00	606·00	1212·00
5,100	51·00	102·00	612·00	1224·00
5,150	51·50	103·00	618·00	1,23600
5,200	52·00	104·00	624·00	1248·00
5,250	52·50	105·00	630·00	1260·00
5,300	53·00	106·00	636·00	1272·00
5,350	53·50	107·00	642·00	1284·00
5,400	54·00	108·00	648·00	1296·00
5,450	54·50	109·00	654·00	1308·00
5,500	55·00	110·00	660·00	1320·00
5,550	55·50	111·00	666·00	1332·00
5,600	56·00	112·00	672·00	1344·00
5,650	56·50	113·00	678·00	1356·00
5,700	57·00	114·00	684·00	1368·00
5,750	57·50	115·00	690·00	1380·00
5,800	58·00	116·00	696·00	1392·00
5,850	58·50	117·00	702·00	1404·00
5,900	59·00	118·00	708·00	1416·00
5,950	59·50	119·00	714·00	1428·00
6,000	60·00	120·00	720·00	1440·00
6,050	60·50	121·00	726·00	1452·00
6,100	61·00	122·00	732·00	1464·00
6,150	61·50	123·00	738·00	1476·00
6,200	62·00	124·00	744·00	1488·00
6,250	62·50	125·00	750·00	1500·00
6,300	63·00	126·00	756·00	1512·00
6,350	63·50	127·00	762·00	1524·00
6,400	64·00	128·00	768·00	1536·00
6,450	64·50	129·00	774·00	1548·00
6,500	65·00	130·00	780·00	1560·00
6,550	65·50	131·00	786·00	1572·00
6,600	66·00	132·00	792·00	1584·00
6,650	66·50	133·00	798·00	1596·00
6,700	67·00	134·00	804·00	1608·00
6,750	67·50	135·00	810·00	1620·00
6,800	68·00	136·00	816·00	1632·00
6,850	68·50	137·00	822·00	1644·00
6,900	69·00	138·00	828·00	1656·00
6,950	69·50	139·00	834·00	1668·00
7,000	70·00	140·00	840·00	1680·00
Exceeding £7,000	50p for every £50 or part of £50	£1 for every £50 or part of £50	£6 for every £50 or part of £50	£12 for every £50 or part of £50

5. Leases: Premiums

For duty charged at conveyance rates on premiums, see *ante*, p. 99. Special rates dependent on the inclusion of a certificate of value are not available where the rent exceeds £150 per annum.

6. Instruments executed on or after 1st January, 1892, but before 1st May, 1974

The table below shows the rates of duty applicable between 1st January, 1892, and 30th April, 1974 (inclusively), according to date of execution. Duty was calculated at £5 intervals up to £25 rent, then at £25 intervals up to £100 rent, but thereafter at £50 intervals.

Date of Execution	TERM OF LEASE		
	Not exceeding 35 years or indefinite	Exceeding 35 years but not exceeding 100 years	Exceeding 100 years
1st January, 1892 to 28th April, 1910	£½%	£3%	£6%
29th April, 1910 to 31st July, 1947	£1%	£6%	£12%
1st August, 1947 to 31st July, 1963	£2%* or if rent does not exceed £100 and no consideration in addition to rent £1%	£12%*	£24%*

* Not applicable where the letting is made or agreed to be made to a body of persons established for charitable purposes only or to the trustees of a trust so established. In such cases the rates of duty in force before 1st August, 1947, remain applicable provided the instrument is adjudicated.

Date of Execution	TERM OF LEASE			
	Not exceeding 7 years or indefinite	Exceeding 7 years but not exceeding 35 years	Exceeding 35 years but not exceeding 100 years	Exceeding 100 years
1st August, 1963 to 31st July, 1972	25p per £50 or part of £50 but exempt if rent not exceeding £100	50p for every £50 or part of £50	£3 for every £50 or part of £50	£6 for every £50 or part of £50
1st August, 1972 to 30th April, 1974	As above, but exempt if rent not exceeding £250	As above	As above	As above

Premiums : In the case of leases at a rent and a premium the premium bore duty at the rates applicable to a conveyance on sale (*ante*, p. 99) subject to the following qualifications :—

(i) The special rate introduced on 29th April, 1910, for conveyances containing a certificate of value did not apply to premiums under leases executed before 31st March, 1911 ;

(ii) the special rates dependent on the inclusion of a certificate of value in instruments executed between 31st March, 1911, and 31st July, 1958, inclusive, did not apply where the rent exceeded £20 per annum ;

(iii) the special rates dependent on the inclusion of a certificate of value in instruments executed between 1st August, 1958, and 31st July, 1972, inclusive, did not apply where the rent exceeded £50 per annum ;

(iv) the special rates dependent on the inclusion of a certificate of value in instruments executed between 1st August, 1972, and 30th April, 1974, did not apply where the rent exceeded £150 per annum.

" *Particulars Delivered* " *Stamp, etc.* : see heading no. 3, *ante*, p. 112.